CHATHAM HOUSE PAPERS

OPTIONS FOR BRITISH FOREIGN POLICY IN THE 1990s

CHATHAM HOUSE PAPERS

General Series Editor: William Wallace

Chatham House Papers are short monographs on current policy problems which have been commissioned by the Royal Institute of International Affairs. In preparing the paper, authors are advised by a study group of experts convened by the RIIA. Publication of the paper by the Institute indicates its standing as an authoritative contribution to the public debate.

The Royal Institute of International Affairs is an independent body which promotes the rigorous study of international questions and does not express opinions of its own. The opinions expressed in this publication are the responsibility of the authors.

CHATHAM HOUSE PAPERS

OPTIONS FOR BRITISH FOREIGN POLICY IN THE 1990s

Christopher Tugendhat
and William Wallace

The Royal Institute of International Affairs

Routledge
London and New York

First published 1988
by Routledge
11 New Fetter Lane, London EC4P 4EE
29 West 35th Street, New York, NY 10001

Reproduced from copy supplied by
Stephen Austin and Sons Ltd, Hertford,
Printed in Great Britain by
Billing & Sons Ltd, Worcester

British Library Cataloguing-in-Publication Data

Tugendhat, Christopher, 1937–
    Options for British foreign policy in the
    1990s. (Chatham House papers. ISSN
    0143–5795).
    1. Great Britain. Foreign relations.
    Policies of government – Forecasts
    I. Title   II. Wallace, William, 1941–
    III. Royal Institute of International
    Affairs   IV. Series
    327.41

    ISBN 0–415–00214–1

CONTENTS

Acknowledgments/vii
1 Introduction/1
2 The historical legacy/9
3 The current position/22
4 The economic dimension/35
5 The security dimension/60
6 The intangible elements of foreign policy/82
7 Constraints and choices/104
Notes/120

ACKNOWLEDGMENTS

This paper grew out of the vigorous discussions within a study group convened by the Royal Institute of International Affairs, which met over the winter of 1986–7. We are very grateful to Peter Nailor and Roderic Lyne for guiding the study group and for providing initial drafts around which to focus the discussions. Participants in the study group came from a wide range of backgrounds and political perspectives. We would be astonished if they agreed with every paragraph in this paper, written after the decisive results of the 1987 general election, and revised in the light of further comments and criticisms in the spring of 1988. But we hope that they will both recognize the themes which they contributed and be provoked by the points with which they disagree to carry the debate further forward.

We have benefited from the comments and criticisms of a number of friends and colleagues on successive drafts. For Chapter 4 we drew extensively on DeAnne Julius's paper for the study group, which has since appeared in *International Affairs*, Summer 1987. Kate Grosser provided updated and additional statistics. For Chapter 5 we drew upon a so far unpublished paper by Phil Williams on 'British Defence Policy, Anglo-American Relations and Nato'. Helen Tomkys assembled much of the material and the statistics for Chapter 6. The Institute library and press library repeatedly chased up source material and checked dates, quotations and references. Marie Lathia managed the manuscript through successive drafts. Sophie Witter improved its quality and imposed editorial order. But we alone are responsible for the views expressed.

July 1988   C.T.
                                                                            W.W.

1
INTRODUCTION

The results of the 1987 general election appear to have settled, for some time to come, many of the underlying questions of British foreign policy. Britain is now an established member of the European Community, involved in an ever-broadening pattern of cooperation – through the EC and through other multilateral networks – on international trade and monetary policies, the prevention of terrorism and drug-smuggling, East-West relations and defence. It retains a close – perhaps even a 'special' – relationship with the United States. It is proceeding, with the help of the United States, to construct and deploy a strategic nuclear deterrent force intended to be in service well into the next century. It will continue to accept its responsibilities as a member of the Atlantic Alliance and will contribute as for many years past to the maintenance of international order in crises outside the Nato area.

After the alarms and excursions of the pre-election debate, the outlines of British foreign policy now seem clear. In contrast to previous elections, Labour accepted in 1987 that Britain could not be disentangled from the European Community. The Labour challenge, radical and destabilizing as it appeared to many, was aimed primarily at the nuclear dimension. Labour spokesmen underlined their commitment to Nato and to Western defence in general, including the maintenance of British defence spending at its current level. The Liberal-SDP Alliance differed from the Conservatives only in emphasis: in its greater enthusiasm for West European cooperation, its relative lack of confidence in the long-term stability

1

of the transatlantic relationship and its reluctant – even ambivalent – acceptance of Britain's nuclear deterrent. Public opinion appeared to respond well to the Conservative emphasis on Britain's 'new strength and new pride', as Mrs Thatcher called it in her introduction to the party manifesto, 'founded on a strong economy and a robust defence'. 'We have not only rebuilt our economy and re-established our world reputation,' the manifesto continued; 'we have also regained our national self-respect.'

British foreign policy now has a firm domestic base of widespread – though not universal – public support. Its main thrust would be instantly recognizable to Harold Macmillan, who, when prime minister, was working towards the same reorientation until the collapse of Britain's first application to join the European Community in January 1963. Except for the greater emphasis on Western Europe and the diminished emphasis on the global and Commonwealth dimension, it would indeed be familiar to those who shaped the last explicit conceptual framework for British foreign policy – the doctrine of 'the three circles', expounded by Winston Churchill at the end of World War II, which argued that Britain's global status was to be maintained through its focal position in the three overlapping 'circles' of transatlantic relations, the British Empire and Commonwealth, and Western Europe. The sense of continuity was underlined during the election campaign by the Prime Minister's association of Britain's re-established role in Europe with the leading part it played in liberating Europe during World War II; film footage of the Normandy beaches in 1944 appeared in the Conservatives' final campaign broadcast.

A world transformed
Yet the world in which Britain makes its foreign policy has changed very considerably since 1945 and is continuing to change now. Some twenty-five years ago Kenneth Younger, then director of the Royal Institute of International Affairs (RIIA), published an essay on *Changing Perspectives in British Foreign Policy*, in which he questioned whether the British government had taken sufficient account of the shifting nature of the US-British special relationship and concluded that Britain 'should not aim to prolong a privileged status among the allies of the United States'.[1] He noted the increasing importance of West Germany to Britain's political, economic and

security concerns; the gradual but steady drift away from the bitter confrontation of the cold war towards a more open relationship between the two halves of Europe; and the implications of France's development of an independent deterrent for the future of the British nuclear force. He argued that Nato should not be considered an unchanged or unchanging part of the international landscape, nor the US commitment of substantial conventional forces to Europe a permanent feature. He saw Britain's continuing security commitments outside Europe as a post-imperial hangover, which tended 'to perpetuate Britain's deeply ingrained belief that she has a destiny which separates her from other industrial nations of similar size and power'.[2] He criticized the preoccupation with the international role of sterling and Britain's leading international financial position, and pressed for a multilateral approach to economic, industrial and scientific cooperation. 'Various circumstances have delayed for a generation or more', he observed, 'the consequences to Britain of the emergence of advanced industrial powers far larger than herself in area, population and resources. The delay is now at an end and certain choices have to be made.'[3] In arms production, aircraft manufacture, nuclear power and space research Britain would have to find partners if it wished to maintain a capability, and this partnership would 'probably be more often "found" inside the European Community than with outsiders'.[4]

Younger was writing in a period which he and others saw as the end of the postwar era, marked by a shift from the bilateralism of a superpower confrontation to the multilateralism of a more complex international order, in which the wider distribution of economic strength and the disappearance of colonial empires was dispersing power among a larger number of governments and international institutions. Many of the questions he posed remain directly relevant today, not yet resolved by the evolution of British policy or external events. The Atlantic Alliance has proved more stable than he and others feared, surviving the crisis of de Gaulle's root-and-branch challenge without major reform. But the problems which had been thrown up by German rearmament and by the loss of American strategic invulnerability, successfully papered over in the mid-1960s, have now resurfaced. The Berlin crises of 1958–61 brought additional American troops to central Europe, reinforcing a commitment which had not been intended as permanent. Today the scale and scope of the US military commitment, and the way in which the burden of defence is shared between the Europeans and the Americans, are matters of anxious debate on both sides of the Atlantic. The problem of choosing partners, and of the appropriate degree of government sponsorship, in civil and military research, development and manufacture, are still with us, as evidenced by the rifts in the Cabinet over the future of Westland and the British contribution to Airbus Industrie.

But much that Younger could assume as shared between those who set the guidelines for British foreign policy after the war and those – both in and outside the government – who were attempting to reshape them in the early 1960s has ceased to obtain in the second half of the 1980s. He took it as given that central Europe was *the* focus of global strategy, as demonstrated by the recurrent crises over the status of Berlin. He recognized that the recovery of Western Europe had made transactions among the industrialized countries on either side of the Atlantic the fulcrum of the international economy. He did not envisage problems of energy security for an industrialized world which was moving from dependence on coal to a bright future of nuclear power, with cheap and plentiful oil as a stop-gap on the way. He paid little attention to the Arab countries, apart from Aden and the Trucial Gulf states, to which Britain was politically and militarily committed. He briefly noted China as a factor in the global security balance and made one passing reference to Japan as an industrializing country.

The world is no longer such a comfortably Eurocentric place. The 'arc of crisis' for global security now stretches from Israel, through Lebanon, Syria and Iraq, to the Gulf, Iran and Afghanistan. Islam is a force with which the 'Christian' world must now reckon, and which has a significant presence in Britain itself, as well as in Germany, France and, of course, the Soviet Union. The strategic confrontation between the US and the USSR now takes place across the Arctic and the northern Pacific as much as across the north German plain. The Pacific is beginning to replace the Atlantic as the fulcrum of the international economy. Seen from Tokyo and Los Angeles, Western Europe lies at the far end of the Eurasian continent, on the outer edges of the Japanese and American world-view. West European governments are concerned to maintain European industrial and technological competitiveness against the dynamic interaction of the Japanese and American economies. London has, it is true, successfully maintained – even strengthened –

its position as an international financial centre, but it has now been transformed into the European leg of a global financial triad with Tokyo and New York. Decolonization has left behind a scattering of awkward issues: southern Africa the most intractable, the Falklands, Gibraltar and Hong Kong. But the less developed world now troubles Britain's public and policy-makers in different ways, ranging from famine, refugees and the persistent pressures of immigration to the destabilizing overhang of international debt.

Western Europe itself has shrunk, in terms of relative population and economic weight. It has shrunk also as a result of the integration which follows from improved communications, more intensive trade, and the homogenization of consumer tastes and political and social ideas. British ministers travel as a matter of course to Brussels, Paris and Bonn and back in a day, with waves of officials in their wake and with little more difficulty than American politicians experience in travelling between, say, New York, Boston, Chicago and Washington. After fifteen years as a member of the European Community and participant in the foreign policy deliberations of European Political Cooperation (EPC), consultation and bargaining have become second nature to a wide swathe of British policy-makers. Kenneth Younger's nephew, George Younger, Defence Secretary since 1986, has been a committed supporter of close European collaboration in defence and arms production, working through the revived Western European Union (WEU) and through other bilateral and multilateral channels to strengthen the European pillar within the Atlantic Alliance. Millions of businessmen, holiday-makers and students surge through Europe's airports and along its motorways, together with a less welcome sprinkling of soccer hooligans, drug-traffickers, organized criminals and terrorists, whom European governments work closely together to combat and control. Britain is far more closely linked to the European continent, by economic, financial, political and social ties, than it was some twenty-five years ago. But at the same time it has developed important connections with the other centres of the industrialized world: it is the European base for American and Japanese international banks, the main gateway to Europe for floods of North American and East Asian students and tourists, the largest foreign investor in the American economy and an important recipient in its turn of US and Japanese investment.

Does Britain need an international strategy?
There has been no coherent reformulation of the principles and priorities of British foreign policy in terms of a national strategy since the 'three circles' doctrine of over forty years ago. The pragmatic tradition of British politics – the lack of concern for precise language, concepts and strategy – contrasts with the overarching doctrines beloved by successive American presidents or pronounced by General de Gaulle. Britain has no annually published government statement on foreign policy, comparable to the Defence White Paper. The speeches of successive foreign secretaries in parliamentary foreign affairs debates range widely over recent developments without forcing them into any overall conceptual scheme.

The prudent approach to British foreign policy was spelt out by Eyre Crowe in his 1907 Memorandum, which argued that Britain's worldwide interests were best protected by a policy that 'is so directed as to harmonize with the general desires and ideas common to all mankind, and more particularly that ... is closely identified with the primary and vital interests of a majority, or as many as possible, of the other nations'. If it was best for Britain to listen to others rather than to attempt to impose its own approach on an unwilling world eighty years ago, the force of that argument may appear far stronger today. Britain is no longer an imperial power, capable of imposing its will across wide regions of the world. It remains an important and diplomatically active state, but it should perhaps accept that stubborn resistance to international trends is no longer an open option.

Foreign policy before World War I was a discrete area of government activity, largely handled by professional diplomats, reporting confidentially to ministers, with only the occasional eruption of popular outrage to disturb the flow of business. Popular attention remains intermittent, with a prevailing lack of interest in global issues being interrupted by the occasional mobilization of public opinion over issues such as the Ethiopian famine, when television, the churches and the Band Aid campaign combined to raise mass awareness. There are, however, more enduring factors that cut across many of the most important aspects of national life. Multinational companies and international banks reach out from Britain to over a hundred countries and into almost every British high street and industrial estate. British holiday-makers travel the world in numbers unimaginable to the aristocratic few who undertook the Grand Tour. Satellite access and regulation, international broadcasting, air and sea pollution and sports all crowd the government's international agenda. No single framework for foreign policy can hope to accommodate so diverse an agenda, or to provide guidelines appropriate to the hundreds of multilateral and bilateral negotiations in which British representatives are at any time engaged. Far better, it is argued, to approach each subject case by case without the unnecessary baggage of ideological predisposition.

Yet in practice such predispositions are unavoidable. If they are not made explicit, they are nevertheless implicit as working assumptions and shared values. The present Conservative government has indeed made the values and assumptions which underlie its approach to foreign policy more explicit than its immediate predecessors. It has recognized, too, the close links between foreign policy, political values and such imprecise but nevertheless undeniable concepts as national identity and national purpose. It has shown itself willing to mount a stubborn resistance to the drift of international trends where these appeared to threaten national identity or national standing – most vividly in its reaction to the Argentine invasion of the Falklands, but also in its sustained resistance to putting the pound sterling within the exchange-rate mechanism of the European Monetary System (EMS). Although the Prime Minister and the Foreign Secretary have not propounded any self-conscious 'grand design', it is clear that they wish to reassert Britain's role in the world, and to do so in a way of which Harold Macmillan would have approved: by asserting a leading role in Europe, maintaining a special relationship with the United States, and cultivating close personal relations with American and Soviet leaders. The Commonwealth, however, is no longer accorded the significance it held in Macmillan's day, as a third stage on which British leaders might play a central role.

In what follows, we consider first the historical legacy which forms the context for current policy and which has shaped and reshaped the implicit assumptions of successive governments. We then examine different dimensions of external policy, looking at Britain's current approaches and obligations, at the policies of some

7

analogue governments, and at the international environment in which policy has to be made. Finally we set out a number of propositions about the range of choices open to British policy-makers over the next few years, and suggest some shifts in the balance of current policy which we believe to be in Britain's long-term interest.

2
THE HISTORICAL LEGACY

Foreign policy is unavoidably bound up with a nation's view of itself. The larger and more powerful the country, the more important the idea of its international role as a part of its national myth. When Anthony Eden expressed his resistance to a closer relationship with the European continent by referring to our 'island story', when Hugh Gaitskell called up '1,000 years of history', they were both saying that the history of England and their sense of identity as Englishmen implied a certain conception of foreign policy – and excluded other theoretical alternatives. The current government has sought both to adapt and to reinforce the sense of a British tradition and a British role.

Britain has had the good fortune not to have been faced with sharp discontinuities in its modern history, or with the painful process of coming to terms with defeat, division or dishonour. It has been spared the agonies of French reinterpretation of the record of resistance and collaboration during World War II, the trauma of the Spanish Civil War and its aftermath, the national (and personal) agonies of Germany and Austria in coming to terms with what happened under Hitler, or the ambivalence of the Italian state tradition. British history, as popularly understood, is the story of the extension of English ideas and influence, of the sustained defence of liberty against Continental despotism, of the benign character of the nineteenth-century *Pax Britannica*, and of the maturing of Empire into a free association of states. World War II reinforced this tradition, adding to it the strong sense of a community of ideas and sentiment among all the English-speaking people which gave Britain the international standing that it could no longer have maintained on its own.

It is less easy to construct an agreed account of the evolution of British foreign policy since 1945. For some, the baggage of the past has weighed Britain down with post-imperial assumptions and commitments, distracting its leaders from the need to face up to Britain's sharply reduced economic and political strength. But for most, withdrawal from Empire and accommodation to the European continent has been a gradual but successful process, completed without large-scale colonial wars or domestic disruption, maintaining the basic traditions of British foreign policy and leaving Britain with a valuable legacy in terms of its international reputation.

The postwar partnership
Britain emerged from World War II as one of 'the Big Three'. But after the tenacity with which it and its Empire had maintained the struggle against the Axis powers, with domestic resources and overseas assets fully mobilized, the disparity in power between it and the two dominant victors, the US and the USSR, was now beyond argument. Even in Europe the American military contribution in men and *matériel* outstripped the British; in the war against Japan the discrepancy was far greater. Economically, it needed only the abrupt ending of Lend-Lease in the autumn of 1945 to dramatize the extent of British dependence on outside aid.

Yet there were a number of factors which, if they no longer diverted attention from Britain's changed circumstances, nevertheless postponed for a decade or more the moment when Britain would be forced to take stock systematically of what these new circumstances implied, and of what options were left open to it. The most important of these factors was simply the general chaos in which the world found itself and, in particular, the virtually total collapse or exhaustion of so many of the other former great powers. Even the Soviet Union's ability to affect events directly outside its own boundaries was limited to Eastern Europe. The United States was at that time the only true world power, but Britain, given its continuing international responsibilities, came indisputably second. Its ability to discharge these responsibilities might be limited, but it felt itself to have the same sort of international influence that it had had before; its efforts and eventual success in the war could have had no other consequence. Handicapped though it was by lack of resources, it was still cast for a world role which, for the time being, no other power could play in its stead. The shape of the postwar international order and international economy was in many important ways an Anglo-American creation: the International Monetary Fund (IMF) and the World Bank directly reflected British and American discussions; the United Nations and its associated agencies emerged from negotiations in which the British and American participants played a leading part.

The early postwar years saw a number of pragmatic contrivances that amounted to a transfer of responsibilities from Britain to the US, notably in the Mediterranean and the Levant. They also saw the first and decisive stage in the transformation of British imperial responsibilities into the vaguer duties owed to an independent, and diffuse, Commonwealth. After a short period around the end of the war, when the US was inclined to see the British Empire as one of the obstacles to the creation of an appropriately modern world order, the wartime pattern of Anglo-American collaboration was re-established in a period of effective partnership – though this partnership was never as untroubled as it is now often presented. Stalin's policies in Europe had, by 1948–9, re-created Anglo-American military solidarity; Britain was the only ally which had any substantial military capability to bring to America's support. The shift in American policy to global containment, which followed the 'loss' of China and the outbreak of the Korean War, reinforced Britain's position as America's partner; it contributed a Commonwealth division and significant naval forces in Korea, successfully contained communist insurgents in Malaya, and maintained international order and security from Suez to Singapore.

So, in the decade after 1945 the energies of Britain's foreign policy-makers were absorbed by these two tasks: the containment of Soviet military power, particularly in Western Europe, and preparations for the gradual transformation from Empire to Commonwealth. For both, American support and cooperation were indispensable, and for both they were forthcoming – as Britain's policies also clearly served American interests. Mistakes there may have been, in planning as in execution, and there were repeated differences on specific issues between London and Washington. But in broad conception these policies were right, and they were an important contribution to world stability. Throughout the decade after 1945 there was, therefore, a real Anglo-American partnership, to which the British contributed a great deal.

Nevertheless, these necessary preoccupations served to perpetuate, and even enhance, an element in the British attitude to world affairs which, in the long run, has been detrimental: namely, its sense of separateness from Europe. The historical causes of this deeply ingrained feeling were accentuated in the war years; Britain alone among the combatants kept its political and physical integrity while Europe was under hostile control, and the friendly reality was the English-speaking world. The Russians, though often admired, were too remote to arouse an equal feeling of solidarity. The organization of postwar defence began in the European context with the Treaties of Dunkirk and Brussels; but having lived through the 1930s, when guarantees and commitments had been too long withheld, British policy-makers wanted to make sure that the US was committed to an active defence of Europe. When this goal was achieved by the creation of Nato in 1949, it was the Anglo-American link to which Britain accorded priority.

This was neither wrong nor parochial, for Nato as a whole undoubtedly depended upon American support. In 1949 the US enjoyed not only a monopoly of nuclear weapons, but also an enormous preponderance of maritime forces and a huge reserve of economic and material resources. But a largely unintentional by-product of this policy was a prolongation of the perception, both on the Continent and in Britain, that, within the Atlantic Alliance, the Continent was one thing and North America and Britain were another – just as they had been between 1940 and 1945. George Orwell reflected this view of the world when in *Nineteen eighty-four* he included Britain, as 'Airstrip One', in American-dominated Oceania rather than with the Continent in Eurasia. This perception, however, was never as strong in Washington, where supporters of European unity within the Western Alliance saw Britain as a necessary part of a united Europe.

Two new trends supported the old Atlantic links. The first was the development of the nuclear weapons industry and the American attitude to the sharing of nuclear secrets. Britain was denied the benefits of continued cooperation with America in nuclear matters by the MacMahon Act of 1946, and so it decided to renew its own national programme of development. It was far ahead of the rest of Europe in the field of nuclear power, and was able to manufacture its own weapons; in due course it made enough progress to qualify for favourable treatment under American legislation of the late 1950s. This, coming on top of both the intelligence-sharing arrangements between London and Washington and the close consultation which wartime experience and habit still assured to British service chiefs in America, placed Britain in a uniquely privileged position alongside the overwhelmingly powerful Americans. The Anglo-American domination of the new Nato organizations reinforced this alignment.

The second trend was the growth of the movement towards European unity. The breakdown of European national institutions between 1939 and 1945, coming as it did after the turbulence of the years since 1914, stimulated a belief on the Continent which was both rational and instinctive: that Europe had to organize itself supranationally if it was to avoid being torn apart again in further wars. This sentiment, however, was not – perhaps could not be – fully shared by Britain; its political culture and traditions were so far removed from the preoccupations of such men as Adenauer, De Gasperi and Schuman, whose ideology was Roman Catholic and Christian Democratic, and whose political experience was infused with concern for the borderlands of Latin and German culture: the Rhineland, the Tyrol, Lorraine. While Britain might encourage and applaud the movement towards unity, its own national preoccupations lay elsewhere.

In opposition Winston Churchill had sounded a warmer note on the theme of West European cooperation, in reaction against a Labour government which was instinctively wary of the European Catholic parties. But the Conservatives, on their return to office in 1951, were no less wary of the proposals for a European Defence Community than their predecessors had been of the European Coal and Steel Community – in spite of strong American support for both initiatives. Of the 'three circles' in the conceptual framework of British foreign policy, Western Europe was seen as the one from which Britain gained least, and to which it was forced to make the heaviest contribution – in contrast to the clear benefits it gained from the transatlantic partnership, and the continuing prestige which the British Commonwealth offered. On the collapse of the European Defence Community proposals in 1953, and under intense

American pressure, the British government was nevertheless forced to enter into a long-term, peacetime, Continental commitment, pledging itself in the 1954 WEU Treaty to maintain four divisions and a tactical air force in West Germany; this was a key element in the framework which enabled France and the Benelux countries to accept German rearmament.

The experience of the 1950s did much to increase Britain's sense of difference from its Continental neighbours. Its stable and self-confident democracy contrasted with the unstable and short-lived coalitions of France and Italy. The British were largely spared the civil disorder and the social divisions which the presence of powerful communist parties and communist-led unions implied across the Channel. Their experience of disengagement from Empire, though marked by repeated 'emergencies' in Malaya, Kenya, Cyprus, Aden and Borneo, was happier than that of France, whose retreat from Indochina was followed by the Algerian War and the collapse of the Fourth Republic. The one episode in which the British government chose partnership with France rather than with the United States came in the 1956 Franco-British military intervention on the Suez Canal. The impact of American disapproval, the threat of Soviet nuclear blackmail, and the renewed revelation of economic vulnerability was painful for both countries. But the aftermath drove them in different directions: the British to re-establish a close relationship with the Americans; the French to intensify their efforts to build an alternative base for support, by harnessing West German economic strength to French objectives through close European cooperation.

From Suez to Nassau
Britain's immediate response to the humiliation of Suez focused on two areas: the Anglo-American relationship and Britain's defence capacity. Macmillan's success in re-establishing mutual confidence between the transatlantic partners was underlined by the 'Declaration of Interdependence', which he and President Eisenhower issued in Bermuda in October 1957. But the old pattern could not be entirely restored. In Washington the sense both of mutual benefit and of respect for British experience in world affairs was weaker; in London the sense of dependence upon the goodwill of a more powerful patron was more acute.

The 1957 British defence review was already under way at the time of the Suez intervention. The crisis had a strong impact on the presentation of policy, with a heavy emphasis being placed on the independent nuclear deterrent as the symbol and guarantor of Britain's world status. Where the 1956 White Paper had called the British force 'a contribution to the Allied deterrent', the 1957 White Paper noted that it would give Britain 'an appreciable element of nuclear power of her own'. The conventional commitment to maintain substantial forces East of Suez was to be sustained, after the loss of the Canal Zone base, by the expansion of bases in Kenya (and later in Aden) and Singapore. The number of British forces in Germany was, however, to be reduced – only three years after the WEU commitment – from 70,000 to 45,000, a figure later adjusted to 55,000 after much hard bargaining over support costs with the German government, and in the face of sustained American pressure. The review successfully contained the rising costs of defence, but was unable to reduce the proportion of defence expenditure to government spending as much as some ministers had hoped.

The experience of Suez also gave added impetus to the pace of disengagement from Empire. Ghana, the first of Britain's African colonies to gain self-government, was already on the path towards independence, which it achieved in 1957. Preparations for self-government in Britain's other African territories were speeded up. In those with European settler populations, this shift in priorities imposed strains which carried through to British domestic politics, as first in Kenya and then in Central Africa the metropolitan government moved towards majority rule. Harold Macmillan's 1960 'winds of change' speech and the consequent South African withdrawal from the Commonwealth were part of this process of disengagement, of adjusting British objectives and ambitions to reduced capabilities and to a changing international environment.

The most difficult arena for adjustment was in relations with the European continent. Britain's response to the revival of Continental efforts for closer union, through a European common market, had been to counter-propose a plan for a wider and looser free trade area based on the Organization for European Economic Cooperation (OEEC, later to become the OECD). Negotiations on this were at a crucial stage when the 1957 Defence White Paper announced the reduction of British ground and air forces in Germany. When 'the Six' went ahead to sign the Treaties of Rome, setting up European Economic and European Atomic Energy Communities, Britain was left to lead an alternative European Free Trade Area which brought together the more hesitant nations around the periphery.

British policy-makers had fought hard to avoid being forced to shift priorities from their Atlantic and Commonwealth links to Europe. The bulk of Britain's external trade was still with the United States and the sterling area. The economic advantages of European integration were not self-evident, and the political price in terms of sovereignty seemed unacceptable. British politicians did not share the preoccupation of their Continental neighbours with the containment of Germany's economic and military recovery; they did not see the relevance of calls for political unification through economic integration. Yet the United States, as ministers were aware, strongly favoured the integration of Europe, including Britain, despite the prospect of trade discrimination against the US by the new Europe. It was not disposed to adopt a similar attitude to any purely commercial free trade area which Britain might devise, any more than it had tolerated imperial preferences. It was the prospect of some form of political integration that gave the Community its appeal in Washington, and that might give a foundation to the architectural metaphor of 'two pillars'.

The final strand in the Macmillan government's reassessment of Britain's capabilities and priorities was the reversal of assumptions about the EEC after the 1959 elections, culminating in the application submitted in July 1961. Recognition of the disappointing sluggishness of the British economy, and of the impetus which the common market appeared to be giving to Continental economic growth, was reinforced by awareness of the need for Britain to find partners in civil and military high technology if it was to maintain its place as a military power and an industrial nation of the first rank. The cancellation in 1960 of the Blue Streak missile, on which the British government had hoped to rely for its next generation nuclear deterrent, led both to a request to the US administration to provide the Skybolt stand-off missile as a substitute, and to a British initiative to set up new mechanisms for European cooperation through the European Launcher Development and European Space Research Organizations. Faced with acute difficulties in funding the development of the next generation of civil aircraft, and refusing to accept that Britain should therefore drop out of such a high-prestige field, the government also signed an agreement with the French for joint development of a supersonic transport.

However, the strength and continuity of the British traditions in foreign policy, combined with the shifting priorities of American and French administrations, made it extremely difficult for the Macmillan government to weave together these different strands into a coherent new strategy. If Britain had succeeded in joining the EEC in 1962–3, it could have become a leading partner in building the 'European pillar' of the Atlantic Alliance, alongside France and Germany – still closely linked to the Commonwealth and Washington, but with the European commitment advanced from the last to the first of the three circles of British influence and obligation. Neither parliamentary nor public opinion was prepared for such a decisive shift of priorities. The incompatibility of parliamentary sovereignty with the Roman Law constitutionalism of the Continent, the obligations Britain owed to the Commonwealth countries, and the corporatist and mercantilist approach of Continental governments to economic policy were all seen as objections. But it was the independent deterrent which provoked the collapse of the negotiations. The American cancellation of Skybolt led Macmillan to press President Kennedy at their Nassau meeting to offer the Polaris missile instead. President de Gaulle in response not only rejected the weak offer of technical collaboration with France which accompanied the British application to join the European communities, but also took the opportunity to veto the application itself.

The adjustment to Europe
The collapse of the Macmillan government's application left the American strategy to create a more coherent Atlantic partnership, with an integrated Western Europe assuming a larger share of both the defence burden and the international economic leadership, in disarray. But it left British foreign policy in much greater confusion. While attempting to balance the continuation of a special Anglo-American defence relationship with a more definite political and economic commitment to the European continent, against the background of vigorous lobbying from Commonwealth governments and an unprepared and doubtful domestic public, the government had tripped up over the Skybolt cancellation, to fall on the Atlantic side. All the more wounding, therefore, that the cruellest comment on the outcome should have come from an influential American with long experience of the Anglo-American relationship.

Dean Acheson's remark that 'Britain has lost an Empire but it has not yet found a role' was sharply condemned in Britain precisely because it struck home so accurately. Acheson's more detailed comments were less widely noted. He continued: 'The attempt to play a separate power role – that is a role apart from Europe ... based on a "special relationship" with the United States ... on being the head of a "Commonwealth" which has no political structure, unity or strength ... this role is about played out.'[1]

The gap between aspirations and resources, which had led both to dependence on the USA for the launch vehicle for Britain's deterrent and to the turn towards the European continent for economic and technological cooperation, widened still further during the following decade. The Labour government which was returned to power in 1964 was at the outset strongly committed both to the Anglo-American tie and to the value of the Commonwealth, as against the unfamiliar and potentially irreversible commitments of the European Community. The Nassau Agreement had, after all, reinforced the special military relationship, on advantageous terms; sterling and the dollar retained their links as reserve currencies, in spite of recurring pressures on sterling. In 1964 British troops successfully suppressed mutinies in Tanganyika and Uganda, on the invitation of their governments; other forces were defending Borneo against an Indonesian-inspired insurgency. The new government offered in 1964 to contribute its planned Polaris submarines to an 'Atlantic Nuclear Force', in order to engage the West Germans more closely in the Alliance's nuclear dimension. In 1965 Prime Minister Harold Wilson suggested that two of the submarines should be stationed East of Suez, to offer a nuclear guarantee to India against the threat of another Chinese attack.

Yet economic constraints and external developments hemmed the government in. The TSR-2 (a tactical strike reconnaissance plane intended to be the mainstay of the RAF's strike force, and of military aircraft exports, for the 1970s) was cancelled in a public expenditure review soon after Labour entered office. To fill the gap the government turned to Paris, signing in 1965 an agreement for the joint development of two military aircraft and three types of helicopter. In 1967 the defence of the sterling/dollar parity – seen until then as one of the symbols of Britain's global status – proved beyond the government's capabilities. In the expenditure cuts which followed devaluation the East of Suez commitment was abandoned, the withdrawal to be completed by 1970. As the US administration's preoccupation with Asian security rose, with its growing military commitment to Vietnam, its most important postwar partner was moving away from Asia; this unavoidably reduced Britain's standing in Washington, even as the British government attempted to find a balance between America's demands for more explicit support of its Vietnam policy and domestic discontent with that policy.

The Commonwealth connection was also becoming less appealing. Labour found itself getting little sympathy or help from Commonwealth governments when the disengagement from central Africa culminated in Rhodesia's unilateral declaration of independence in 1965. The restrictions on Commonwealth immigration into Britain, introduced in 1962 and progressively tightened in the face of a rising influx, created other strains – which were exacerbated by the expulsion of Asians from East Africa in the late 1960s, and by the refusal of the Indian government to share the responsibility for accommodating them. The Indian government at this time was more concerned with relations with the superpowers, in particular the Soviet Union, than with its traditional links with Britain, while Australia was following Canada in reorienting itself more towards the United States.

In 1967 the Wilson government renewed Britain's application to join the European Communities. It offered the strengths of British high technology, to be shared within a proposed European technological community, as its 'trump card'; but it met again with de Gaulle's veto. Thereafter Labour's European commitment was maintained through closer links with Federal Germany, with which a number of agreements on joint military procurement were made in 1968–70, and through the shift of Britain's military and security priorities from East of Suez to the European theatre. Britain, Germany, Italy and the Netherlands used the framework of WEU for political consultations, thus circumventing the French veto. The British and West German defence ministers took the initiative to establish the Eurogroup in 1969, to bolster – and to make more visible in Washington – European cooperation within the Atlantic Alliance.

The Heath government, on taking office in 1970, inherited the negotiating brief which Labour had prepared for a renewed application after the resignation and death of de Gaulle. Edward Heath chose to emphasize the Franco-British connection as the key to wider European cooperation, taking advantage of the reorientation of French policy under Pompidou and of French unease over West Germany's growing economic strength and its *Ostpolitik*. Conversations between London and Paris covered foreign policy, industrial and technological coopearation, and potential nuclear collaboration. Negotiations were concluded successfully, and Britain joined the Community in January 1973.

After fifteen years of steady economic growth in the European Community and outside, it was a cruel misfortune that Britain's entry should be accompanied by the onset of an international recession. The disruption caused by international financial instability was compounded by the 1973 Middle East war and sharp rises in oil and commodity prices. The government had decided to enter the Community without tying up every detail of the policy adjustments needed to accommodate British interests, recognizing that the economic costs of Community membership might well prove on existing policies to be higher than the benefits, but trusting to the process of policy-making inside the Community to alter the balance progressively in Britain's favour. It found itself inside a Community distracted by domestic economic difficulties and reluctant to embark on reforms and innovations. The Community's policy-making capacities were further strained, from 1977 on, by a second round of applications for membership, which made the allocation of costs and benefits for the future an ever more complex task.

The Labour government which returned to office in 1974 was internally divided over the European commitment, and it devoted its first year in office to a lengthy and diplomatically disastrous process of 'renegotiation'; this was followed by a national referendum, which produced a decisive result but left behind an unreconciled 'anti-European' grouping with strong support on the left of the Labour Party. The West European balance which emerged in the second half of the 1970s, for this and other reasons, was not centred upon a Franco-British or a German-British understanding, or even upon the triangular 'directorate' for which some had called. Under Chancellor Schmidt and President Giscard d'Estaing the Franco-German relationship became the clear centre of European policy. British policy-makers found themselves competing in Washington with the Germans for attention as the USA's most important European partner, and struggling to redress an adverse financial balance within the European Community without becoming isolated within the multilateral West European game.

The most debilitating factor in the late 1970s was the sense of economic weakness, of Britain's international claim to status becoming increasingly false as its economic position declined. Sir Nicholas Henderson's 'valedictory despatch' on leaving his Paris embassy in 1979 pointed out that 'we are scarcely in the same economic league as Germany and France, . . . so that today we are not only no longer a world power, but we are not in the first rank even as a European one.'[2] Britain had taken longer to adjust its economy to the impact of the 1973–5 upsurge in the price of raw materials than most of its major competitors and had suffered higher levels of domestic inflation. Production of North Sea oil and gas had not yet offered substantial relief from its trade deficit. Ministers took their place alongside their American, French and German colleagues in discussing global security and economic problems, but they were uncomfortably aware of the limits of British influence under such circumstances, and of the attitudes of their partners to 'the British disease'. Prime Minister Callaghan returned from the four-power summit in Guadeloupe in December 1978 to grapple with the upsurge of wage demands and the consequent economic difficulties which marked the 'winter of discontent'.

The mood of disillusionment with foreign policy, as an activity independent of immediate concerns of economic advantage, was articulated most explicitly by the Central Policy Review Staff's *Review of Overseas Representation*. Presenting his report in late 1977, Sir Kenneth Berrill noted:

> In the past 20 years our share of the total Gross Domestic
> Product of the OECD countries has fallen by a quarter and our
> share of world trade has fallen by more than a half. In today's
> world a country's power and influence are basically determined
> by its economic performance. Inevitably therefore the UK's
> ability to influence events in the world has declined and there is
> very little that diplomatic activity and international public rela-
> tions can do to disguise the fact.[3]

3
THE CURRENT POSITION

The perspective of 1988 is far less gloomy. Indeed the most striking aspect of the British government's approach to foreign policy, after the Conservatives' third-term election victory, has been its regained self-confidence. 'Once more', Mrs Thatcher declared to the Conservative Party conference of October 1987, 'Britain is confident, strong, trusted ... Strong, because our economy is enterprising, competitive and expanding. And trusted, because we are known to be a powerful ally and a faithful friend.' Continuity in office, economic recovery, sustained military expenditure, and a robust and assertive style in foreign policy – firmly stamped with the Prime Minister's own personality – have combined to restore a degree of self-assurance greater than that of any government since Suez, perhaps since World War II.

The current mood of self-confidence rests as heavily on an assessment of Britain's underlying economic strength as did the gloom of the 1970s on a perception of weakness. It is our economic success, the Prime Minister argued in her 1987 conference speech, which 'has enabled Britain to play a more prominent role in the world at large. We are now the second biggest investor in the world, and the very model of a stable economy ... We now have a new Britain, confident, optimistic, sure of its economic strength – a Britain to which foreigners come to admire, to invest, yes and to imitate.' The flow of North Sea oil has enabled the government to set about the restructuring of Britain's domestic economy without being held back by balance-of-payments difficulties. It has given it the opportunity, furthermore, to open up protected sectors of the British economy to international competition, in many cases taking unilateral action to remove regulatory barriers. Britain now has one of the most open national economies in an increasingly inter-dependent world, with inward and outward flows of investment considerably higher than those of its neighbours. The appropriate level of government intervention in industry and in external economic policy, and the objectives which such intervention should serve for a government committed to deregulation and open markets, have therefore become matters of some uncertainty and controversy, to be discussed further in Chapter 4.

Much has also been made in the current presentation of British foreign policy of the intangible elements of national standing in the international arena. It is peculiarly difficult to assess the role of ideas, the sense of national character, in international politics. Domestic perspectives rarely fit those from abroad, and the attitudes of one country often differ radically from those of another. 'It is all that is gifted, just and fair in that character which reassures our friends and allies,' Mrs Thatcher assured her party conference. Certainly the British approach to deregulation has been a model which other governments have wished to follow – a notable example being the 'Thatcherite' policies of the Chirac government in France in 1986–8. But the British government has not followed the Ameri-can administration, in its turn, in actively using the instruments available to government to promote its political and social values. Expenditure on the British Council, the BBC External Services and overseas information have been firmly held down. The flow of students from overseas has been limited by the introduction of full-cost charging for most applicants. There is uncertainty and contro-versy over how much government should intervene in the vast and varied exchanges of information, ideas and people between Britain and other countries – particularly since the establishment of English as the leading global language gives private British initiatives a structural advantage in the international market-place. Britain's image abroad, and the part which foreign policy plays in shaping Britain's self-image at home, are explored further in Chapter 6.

The pattern of public expenditure provides a useful indication of underlying assumptions about priorities, in foreign policy as elsewhere. Britain now spends significantly less than France or Germany (where the figures are complicated by substantial Länder expenditure, which supplements federal spending) on support for civil industry in the international context, reflecting the prevailing government assumption that the international economic environment is relatively friendly to British interests, and that market forces will prevail in most cases over mercantilist intervention. It spends proportionately less than any comparable Western country on the promotion of its values, on its cultural inheritance and its educational facilities, in the belief that these assets can sell themselves in the international market without substantial assistance from government. The field in which Britain stands out from its partners is defence, on which its government spends significantly more than all its major allies except the United States, as a proportion of both GDP and public expenditure – and spends more than any other ally except the United States in foreign currency across the exchanges. The rationale for this is examined in Chapter 5.

The style and character of a government may itself contribute much to the strength – or weakness – of a country's international standing. The image of Britain as a major power, with experienced political leaders and a skilled diplomacy, helped to maintain British international influence in the decade after World War II, in spite of its much-depleted economic and military resources. The Suez campaign and its failure shattered that image. The impression which Chancellor Schmidt and other political leaders gained in the 1970s, of a British government unwilling to face up to difficult choices at home or to pursue consistent priorities abroad, reinforced their perception of a country in decline.

One of the assets which British foreign policy now possesses is the image of a determined government, most of all of a robust and experienced prime minister. The transformation of American press coverage of Britain over the past eight years, from pessimistic regret to enthusiasm for Britain's renewed vigour, is a tribute to Mrs Thatcher's international reputation, as well as to the recovery of the British economy. The success of the Falklands campaign – in contrast to the failure of Suez – played a crucial part in the re-establishment of Britain's self-confidence. It demonstrated to other governments, and to their citizens, that Britain now had a government prepared to defend its national interests with all the resources at its disposal, regardless of the drift of 'international opinion'. It restored to the British public a sense of pride in its international standing, and of confidence in the maintenance of national sovereignty. The determination and vigour of the prime minister's campaign to reduce Britain's contribution to the European Community budget, and beyond that to force the pace of reform of the Common Agricultural Policy, reinforced this image of an invigorated country both at home and abroad.

The personal stature and reputation of a prime minister will not, however, transfer to her successor. The impact of the Falklands campaign is already fading, with ministers grappling with more intractable issues, such as the future of Gibraltar and the return of Hong Kong to Chinese sovereignty. British national interests cannot be so vividly characterized or defended in most of the intricate multilateral negotiations now under way or in prospect. The elements of national pride, national standing and national sovereignty – all non-rational and often intangible, but central to the politics of British foreign policy – are discussed further in Chapters 4–7.

Britain's international position has stabilized after many years of retreat from Empire and economic decline. With a growing stock of overseas investment, a level of domestic economic growth above those of many of its competitors, and an impressive contribution to Western security, it remains in 1988 a major state, with attributes of wealth, power and historical connection which give its interests and its actions weight within the international community.

Two questions follow from this assessment. First, what is the political orientation which underpins this position? Second, how stable is the international environment to which this position relates, and what are the dynamic (and potentially destabilizing) forces which might transform it?

The political orientation
Looking back on the uncertainties of the 1970s, one of the most striking aspects of Britain's current position is the extent to which it has become a West European state, first and foremost. Britain has been a member of the European Community for fifteen years. It has been involved in the foreign policy consultations of EPC almost since they began in 1971. The major commitments of its army and air force are to central Europe, of its navy to the North Sea, the English Channel and the eastern Atlantic. Federal Germany vies with the United States as Britain's single most important trading partner. Western Europe as a whole provides over half of Britain's imports, and absorbs over half its exports.

While the Community framework has been a source of much pain and frustration to Britain's representatives on many occasions, EPC has provided a context and a reinforcement for British foreign policy-makers which successive foreign secretaries have come to appreciate – while operating within it has become second nature to their officials. Sir Geoffrey Howe has remarked that he sees his opposite numbers from France, Germany and the other leading European countries more regularly than he sees some of his colleagues in the British Cabinet, as he moves from Community Council of Ministers to EPC ministerial meetings, from European Councils to bilateral exchanges, and from consultations in the margin of Nato Councils to UN General Assemblies.

The shift towards a European framework for British policy has affected more than just foreign policy. All Britain's major political parties have linked themselves into European confederations fighting European elections on loosely agreed platforms. The Conservatives and Labour are well represented in the European Parliament, and in 1986 a British Conservative was elected its president. Energy, air transport, financial deregulation, regional development and manpower training – all these aspects of domestic policy-making have been affected by European considerations, such as Community rules, funding, or negotiations. The European Court of Justice has, through its rulings, managed to further the cause of equal pay for women in Britain.

Yet the European connection has not become a matter for the heart as well as the head. The European Community still has little appeal for most British citizens, or for many of their political leaders, even though they accept it as a necessary framework for British policy. The Community is seen as a forum for hard bargaining in defence of national interests, not as a part of Britain's international *persona*. The Conservatives' 1987 manifesto again summarized the current hard-headed consensus well: 'We will continue to play a responsible leading role in the development of the Community, while safeguarding our essential national interests.'

The relationship with the United States has continued to attract warmth from among the political elite, particularly – but not exclusively – on the right of British politics. Neil Kinnock, as Labour Party leader, travelled twice to Washington in 1986–7 to seek to persuade Reagan of the acceptability of Labour defence policies, without feeling the need to visit either the French president or the

West German chancellor. The 'special relationship' is still seen by most political leaders as of particular value and importance to Britain, in terms both of the specific nuclear and intelligence links and of the more general exertion of British political influence in Washington.

By and large, British and American interests – and, more broadly, West European and American interests – are accepted as complementary and compatible, based on a shared understanding of the stability of the international order and of the main threats to that stability. In the security sphere, Britain shares with the United States a common interpretation of the Soviet threat as the main source of international insecurity, even though it finds itself differing with Washington from time to time on the global or local causes of particular outbreaks of disorder. The Atlantic Alliance therefore remains the essential framework for British and West European security. The contribution of Britain's nuclear deterrent to the common defence is not precisely defined; but the deterrent is seen as a symbol of its security commitment and as an essential factor in ensuring its continued influence within the Alliance, not to mention the final guarantor of its national sovereignty.

It is as widely accepted that Britain, as a major power of the second rank, retains a share of Western responsibility for maintaining international security outside the Nato area. British ships have now maintained a discreet presence in the waters of the Gulf for eight years, alongside the French and the more recently arrived Americans. Britain contributed a token force to the joint American-French-Italian intervention in the Lebanon in 1982, and took part, at the Egyptian government's invitation, in mine-sweeping operations in the Red Sea in the same year. British military missions are at present helping to train forces in several countries in southern Africa and the Middle East.

Britain's economic interests are seen as inextricably bound up with the preservation and strengthening of the open international order which it and the United States designed at the end of World War II. In a number of areas of international economic relations the British government is now obliged to work through the medium of the European Community, negotiating to agree a common Community position before global negotiations can begin. In other areas, particularly in international finance, the United States remains Britain's most important bargaining partner, with bilateral negotiations (on capital reserve ratios for banks, for example) serving Britain's interests well.

The strength of Britain's international standing is underpinned by its privileged position in many formal and informal international groupings, and by the enormous asset of the use of English as the leading international language. Britain is one of the five permanent members of the UN Security Council. Its position as one of the five declared nuclear powers gives it specific responsibilities in the prevention of proliferation and the promotion of arms control. It is one of the international financial Group of Five, and of the Group of Ten; its prime minister is among the seven international leaders who participate in annual international economic summits, whose discussions now extend to fields such as global security. Ease of communication gives British ministers and officials an inherent advantage in the broad and intricate network of multilateral diplomacy, with British drafts often providing the basis for agreement. Shared language, culture and values help to maintain the close relationship with the United States.

The transatlantic and West European circles of British international influence thus provide the two central elements of British foreign policy in the late 1980s. Each is seen as reinforcing the other, with Britain's special relationship with the United States still enabling it to serve in some ways as a bridge between the United States and its European allies. The Commonwealth connection, the third of the postwar 'circles', has, however, shrunk to a residual factor. From the British government's perspective it brings little of tangible benefit. Intangibles – shared language, culture and values – have become less persuasive as democratic government and Common Law have given way to civil or military authoritarianism. Since the unilateral declaration of independence by Rhodesia in 1965, the Commonwealth as a political grouping, moving from conference to conference with the Secretariat providing continuity, has come to focus more and more on the South African issue, with Britain as the target for its partners' frustrated anger. Successive Labour and Conservative prime ministers bore the Commonwealth's complaints with diplomatic tact, devising or accepting new 'initiatives' to address a problem which the Commonwealth as such had no capacity to resolve. It has been part of the more robust style of Mrs Thatcher's government to resist what is seen as the moral blackmail of the Commonwealth countries, to declare *Britain's* independence, too, of the old ties which no longer bind its former dependencies, and so to recognize that the Commonwealth has become a useful framework for conversation which is, however, no longer a major asset to Britain.[1]

A greater willingness to assert national priorities, rather than to assume – as it does in its approach to the international economy – that the operations of the international order are generally favourable to Britain's interests, has been evident also in the government's dealings with global international organizations and global economic development. Britain followed the United States in withdrawing from UNESCO in 1985, in protest against the policies, attitudes and bureaucratic inefficiencies of that organization. The government has critically examined the case for contributions to a number of European and global organizations, rather than accepting them as automatic obligations which flow from Britain's international responsibilities and standing. In similar fashion it has attempted to redirect the emphasis of Britain's aid programme from multilateral subscriptions towards bilateral pledges which more clearly reflect Britain's immediate political and economic interests. But it has proved difficult to shift the balance far within the constraints of a reduced overall programme, given the scale of Britain's obligations as a member of the European Community, the European Development Fund, and the large number of international programmes ranging from the International Development Association to the World Health Organization to the UN Development Programme – for which Britain's contribution is assessed according to its international economic standing, and to which the United States, alongside the other industrial democracies, makes contributions similarly assessed.

How stable an environment?
The stability and continuity of Britain's foreign policy orientation in the late 1980s depends upon the international environment remaining relatively unchanged. It is, however, likely that international conditions will alter considerably over the next decade. Nor can the maintenance of a stable and open international economic order be taken for granted in the light of current trends.

The most predictable and immediate change is that of the person of the US president, after eight years in which the closeness of the

Reagan-Thatcher dialogue has done much to maintain the special character of the US-UK relationship. In 1989 the British government will have to build a new set of personal relations with the incoming administration, and adjust to its distinctive rhetoric and priorities. It is unlikely that any new president, Republican or Democrat, will establish as close a personal relationship with Mrs Thatcher, or with any potential successor as British prime minister. It is probable that long-term trends in American politics and in the recruitment and outlook of the American elite will continue to shift Washington's perceptions away from the Anglo-Saxon connection, which held sway among the generation that remembered World War II. Relations with Britain will remain an important factor in American foreign policy, still perhaps characterized by a particular warmth and feel, but nevertheless in many ways less important than relations with Germany, Israel and Japan. It is, more broadly, open to question whether the political and security links with Western Europe, in which Britain has for the past forty years claimed to play a special role, will continue to remain the first and fundamental preoccupation of American foreign policy for the foreseeable future. The Pacific Ocean and the Western hemisphere, in neither of which Britain can claim any leading role, are recovering the place in American priorities from which they were displaced by the onset of the cold war in central Europe.

Western Europe is no more likely to stand still over the next decade. The European Community is already committed to the goal of a single internal market by 1992, with governments, companies and banks moving to anticipate the consequences of its achievement. The West European system of which Britain is now a part is both a less coherent and a less clearly defined entity than the European Community which Britain reluctantly joined in 1973. Alongside the real, if modest, step forward of the uniform obligations contained in the Single European Act, which was finally ratified in 1987, there proliferates a diverse network of *ad hoc* groups, bilateral and multilateral arrangements among the Community's core members, and closer links with associated non-members like Sweden, Norway and Switzerland.

It is, however, now clear that Federal Germany is the core of the West European system, both in economic and in security terms. The French government has recognized this fact for over twenty-five years, and has made a close link between Paris and Bonn a strategic objective affecting every dimension of its foreign policy. British governments have so far been less certain, despite the weight of Britain's defence commitment to Germany and the growing importance of the German economy to Britain's external trade. The uncertainties of German politics, the central position of Federal Germany in East-West relations, and the contradictions of German economic policy are now becoming the key to the future development of Europe, and the key, therefore, to British influence over the direction and pace of Europe's development. British actions and attitudes can influence the evolution of relations among its Continental partners, but cannot on their own decide the outcome. In a closely integrated multilateral game in which Britain is only the third most important player, after Federal Germany and France, it will have to bargain, to form coalitions with others, and to decide whether it is better to play or to miss a turn.

The Atlantic Alliance and its concomitant, the Soviet threat, have formed a stable framework for Britain's defence and security policy for the past forty years. We are confident that the Alliance will continue well into the twenty-first century, including a substantial American nuclear guarantee. But we do not anticipate that the shape of the Alliance, or its appreciation of the threat posed by the Warsaw Pact, will remain unchanged. The slow but undeniable evolution of the East European states away from total dependence on the Soviet Union towards closer and less hostile relations with their Western neighbours may well be interrupted by national crises; but it is unlikely to be reversed. 'New thinking' on security policy within the Soviet Union has blossomed under Mr Gorbachev, but it did not begin with his ascendancy. The pressures within the USSR for a redirection of spending away from defence, and within the defence budget away from the massive conventional commitment to central Europe, will remain strong whatever the twists and turns within the Soviet political leadership. Within the United States, too, the struggle to reduce both the budget deficit and the external trade deficit will focus critical attention on the size and cost of the American commitment to Europe. Every presidential candidate in the winter of 1987–8 called for America's allies to take over a greater share of the Alliance's defence burden, echoing a theme long familiar in the US Congress.

The achievement in the 1960s of an open international economy with unprecedentedly high and sustained rates of economic growth owed much to the quality of American leadership and to the dominant position of the United States in global trade, finance and investment. The recovery of Western Europe to balance and challenge America's economic position has now been followed by rapid industrialization in East Asia. The efforts of Britain, alongside other leading industrial countries, to substitute collective economic management for US leadership have had only partial success in resisting pressures to reimpose barriers to trade, and in maintaining balanced economic growth. The overhang of international debt, the emergence of massive imbalances of trade between the United States, East Asia and Western Europe, the volatility of international financial markets, all increase the risk of a sharp deterioration in the international economy. Economic recession and economic protection go hand in hand, both signalling the failure of governments to subordinate immediate national concerns to the broader interests of international coordination.

The transformation of the United States from the world's largest international creditor to its largest international debtor is changing the balance of the global economy, with Japan emerging as dominant creditor nation and financial power. The scale of economic adjustment in both countries required to re-establish equilibrium in the foreseeable future is demanding; successful adjustment would carry major implications both for domestic politics and for external policy in the two countries. The intractability of Third World indebtedness offers a further challenge to the capacity of the leading economic powers to adjust international priorities, particularly as the inability of Latin American and African countries to pay for the imports they need depresses demand in the industrialized world. Sluggish growth and structural rigidities in the West German economy present further difficulties to the devising of coordinated policies to maintain international demand, as the United States attempts to reduce its trade deficit.

The international economic environment in which British policymakers will operate is likely, therefore, to be one of considerable uncertainty, with governments actively engaged in multilateral diplomacy both to protect their own interests and to promote their common interests within an increasingly integrated global economy. British governments will be forced to operate both at the European and at the global level, bargaining with their European partners within the more tightly structured framework of the European

Community, and acting with other West European governments to influence US and Japanese policies. The high degree of economic and technological interdependence between the USA and Japan threatens to make their bilateral relationship the fulcrum of international economic relations over the next decade, with Britain and other West European countries working to protect and promote their interests by exercising influence in Washington and Tokyo. Both in the United States and in Japan the image of a triangular set of key economic relationships is now firmly established; Mr Takeshita spoke during his visit to London in May 1988 of the need for 'the trilateral partners of Japan, Europe and the United States' to 'fulfil their respective responsibilities' in fostering world prosperity. In such a model Britain's role is to be played as part of a West European bloc. But the continuing dispersion of financial and industrial capacities among the other countries of East Asia and beyond suggests that the effective reconciliation of national and international priorities, and the maintenance of an open and relatively stable global economy, can be achieved only within a wider framework than that of trilateralism.

Industrial and technological changes will also continue to reshape Britain's domestic economy and its international environment. Barring catastrophic reverses in international economic cooperation, the integration of the British economy into the European and global economies will increase further. The internationalization of business through inward and outward investment, takeovers and mergers; integrated production across national boundaries; developments in global financial markets; all these will reduce still further the autonomy of the British economy, leaving Britain's economic prospects more dependent than ever upon cooperation with other governments in economic policy, and upon the actions of corporate decision-makers and markets across the world.

The apparent continuity of Britain's foreign policy tradition risks leading its government to underestimate the dynamic character of the processes of international integration – financial, industrial, technological, and also social and cultural – and the problems which these processes pose for national governments in the 1980s and 1990s. The very stability and continuity of the Anglo-American relationship, and of the postwar arrangements for European security over the past forty years, similarly inhibit consideration of the possibilities of political change. In the years of retreat from the

1940s to the 1970s, overstretched resources and a weakening economy forced governments to alter the priorities of British foreign policy – not in response to changes in Britain's commitments or in its strategic environment, but in reaction to budgetary crises and external setbacks. The recovery of the domestic economy since 1981, the continuity provided by a government twice re-elected to office, and the personal commitment and prestige of the current prime minister, have allowed the re-establishment of a stable foreign policy framework. But the pace of external change will force the British government to adjust that framework, as it attempts to define and pursue British interests in an interdependent and rapidly changing world.

4
THE ECONOMIC DIMENSION

Three interrelated elements constitute the economic dimension of a country's foreign policy. The first is the strength of its economy relative to those of other countries. The second is the significance of international transactions to the domestic economy: the level of interdependence between that country's economy and those of other countries, in so far as the implications of interdependence require government intervention and support. The interaction between domestic economic trends and international developments sets the policy agenda for governments in foreign economic policy. The third is the cost of foreign policy broadly defined, and its impact upon the national economy.

Britain's international economic standing

The British economy in 1988 is in a stronger position, in terms of international comparisons, than for very many years. Seven years of continuous economic growth have brought about an improvement in Britain's international ranking after the long period of postwar decline. Britain's growth rate averaged 3.1% over the five years 1983–7, well above the EC average of 2.3% (though still lagging behind Japan, at 3.9%, and the US, at 4.0%). Britain's share of world output, which had fallen steadily from the late 1940s to less than 4.5% in 1973, had risen to nearly 5% in 1985. As an exporting nation Britain's position has also stabilized. Its share of world visible trade, which had fallen to 5.2% by 1973, had recovered to 5.3% by

1985 – though the recovery masked a shift in balance from manufactures (in which the UK share of the world market fell from 7% in 1973 to 5.6% in 1985) to primary products, with Britain emerging as a major oil and a marginal grain exporter.[1]

Far more striking has been the strengthening of Britain's position as a key player in international finance and in the two-way flow of international investment. The UK stands out among OECD member states for the size and strength of its financial sector, which accounted for 7.5% of GDP in 1985 (compared with America's 4.7% of GDP). Britain's share of world exports of financial services was 8% in 1985, well ahead of its share of trade in manufactures.[2] The liberalization of London's financial markets has attracted major banks and securities houses from around the world, with Japanese institutions establishing strong positions alongside American and West European. London has established itself as one of the world's three leading global financial markets, alongside New York and Tokyo.

But most impressive is its position as an international investor: the surplus provided by North Sea oil has re-established the pattern set up in the long period of capital surplus prior to World War II, to make the UK second only to the United States in the absolute size of its foreign direct investment assets. In per capita terms, or as a proportion of GNP, Britain is by far the largest holder of overseas assets outside the smaller Opec countries. Earnings from these investments in 1987 contributed more than half as much to the UK current account as total oil exports had at their peak. Net invisible income on the UK's overseas assets, according to one bank analysis, rose by 25% a year in 1981–7.[3] Meanwhile, investment into the UK has also risen. A recent RIIA study estimates that the real value of Britain's outward foreign direct investment increased by £37 billion between 1980 and 1986, while inward foreign direct investment increased by £19 billion.[4]

The relative standing of other countries has also shifted over the past two decades, and will continue to shift. The USA's proportion of world GNP has fallen from 41.5% in 1962 to 29.7% in 1982, while that of Japan has risen from 4.4% to 10.5%. Exact calculations of relative income are hardly possible in an international system of floating exchange rates, but Table 1 provides an indicator of Britain's current position.

Table 1   GDP and GDP per head rank orders, by country, 1986

	Country	Total GDP (US$ billion)		Country	GDP per head (US $)
1	US	4,195	1	Switzerland	20,830
2	Japan	1,963	2	US	17,360
3	West Germany	892	3	Norway	16,730
4	France	724	4	Iceland	16,170
5	Italy	600	5	Japan	16,160
6	Britain	548	6	Denmark	15,990
7	Canada	367	7	Sweden	15,700
8	Spain	229	8	West Germany	14,610
9	Holland	175	9	Finland	14,320
10	Australia	168	10	Canada	14,200
			17	Britain	9,650

Source: *The Economist*, 30 January 1988.

Britain is no longer the key player in the international economy that it was in the years of Anglo-Saxon predominance and of sterling-dollar cooperation after World War II. West Germany is America's leading European trade partner and competitor. It is also the dominant force in the West European economy, accounting in 1986 for some 24% of the GNP of the twelve-country European Community. The importance of Japan for the US economy – as a competitor, supplier and market – is now far greater than that of any European country. The importance of the US market to Japan – and to the other economies of East Asia – is even more evident. In 1986 more than 37% of Japanese exports went to the American market, while 19% of its imports came from the United States. The bilateral relationship between the United States and Japan is both the most intense and the most politically sensitive dimension of the international economy. Britain, which offers the US a much smaller market and retains a much smaller share in the US market (providing 4% of US imports in 1986, compared to West Germany's 6.8%, Canada's 17.7%, and Japan's 22%), has unavoidably less leverage over policy in Washington. Its ministers find themselves ranged alongside their French and Italian colleagues in international economic diplomacy, seeking to influence a dialogue which threatens to become a triangular argument between the United States and the governments of the structural-surplus economies: Federal Germany and Japan.

Britain nevertheless remains an important player, not only because of the size of its economy and its particular importance in international finance, but also because of its position as a member of a number of key groups concerned with the direction and management of international economic policy, in particular the Group of Seven (G-7) and the IMF Group of Ten. It was a mark of how far Britain had slipped from its postwar position as a dominant player in international economic policy that the proposal to establish the seven-power summits in 1974–5 was a Franco-German initiative, with the British and the Italian governments drawn in to give additional European weight in Washington – and, progressively, in Tokyo.[5] One of the underlying issues in British international economic policy since then has been whether British interests are better served by bilateral diplomacy, particularly in Washington, or by concerting Britain's interests with those of its Continental partners to provide a sufficiently authoritative voice in the dialogue with the United States and Japan.

The pattern of Britain's overseas trade has been moving away from its postwar North American and sterling area orientation towards a high degree of interdependence within Western Europe (see Table 2). In 1985 some 63% of Britain's imports came from EC and EFTA countries, and 59% of its exports went to those markets. West Germany and the United States were its leading trade partners. With the Federal Republic the UK was running its largest bilateral trade deficit; with the USA its largest bilateral surplus. Commonwealth countries now accounted for around 11% of UK exports, and 8% of its imports.

The pattern of Britain's financial links is markedly different. British investment abroad has continued to flow most strongly towards the United States, after a brief diversion towards the Continent when Britain joined the European Community in the early 1970s. It has been estimated that some 60% of Britain's total direct overseas assets are located in North America: more than 50% of the new direct investment flowing from Britain between 1977 and 1986 went to the USA and Canada.[6] The United States also remains the dominant foreign investor in Britain, providing more than half the inward flow of direct investment over the same period. The pursuit of European strategies by German, French, Italian and

Table 2   Geographical distribution of UK trade in goods, 1986

Areas	Exports (%)	Imports (%)
Industrial countries	75.8	82.4
US	15.2	9.9
Japan	1.6	5.7
Belgium/Lux.	5.2	4.7
France	8.5	8.5
West Germany	11.7	16.4
Ireland	4.9	3.5
Italy	4.7	5.4
Holland	7.5	7.7
EC total	48.1	51.8
Developing countries	22.2	15.2
Africa	3.7	3.0
Asia	6.2	5.5
Europe	2.9	2.7
Middle East	7.3	2.0
Rest of world	2.0	2.4

Source: International Monetary Fund, *Direction of Trade Statistics, 1987 Yearbook.*

Swedish companies, which has become a marked feature of Continental investment flows in the late 1980s, seems so far to have passed Britain by; few British companies have yet seen European growth rates as sufficiently attractive, or the prospect of a single internal market as sufficiently compelling. The distribution of Britain's trade in services has also remained largely non-European. The proportion of the UK's total exports of services going to the EC had indeed fallen from 33% in 1973 to 26% in 1985, partly reflecting the EC's lack of progress in liberalizing invisible trade.

Britain's links with Japan are also much stronger in finance and investment than in trade. Over the past ten years Britain has ranked first among West European countries as a host for Japanese investment, notably in electronics and automobiles; however, the total Japanese investment remains small in comparison with the Swedish, Dutch or Italian presence in the British economy. Britain today contains the second largest population of Japanese resident abroad, after the United States, working both in London's Japanese financial institutions and in Japanese-owned companies elsewhere in Britain. British banks represent the largest European presence in Tokyo, and British insurers and other service companies are actively pursuing Asian markets. But Britain trails behind Germany in terms of visible exports to Japan. Italy, the Netherlands and Sweden are all more significant trade partners for Britain than Japan – although after West Germany Japan accounts for Britain's largest bilateral trade deficit.

The changing composition of Britain's trade is also of interest. Oil has been one of the most important of Britain's exports since the late 1970s, accounting for around 20% of visible trade. The balance between manufactured imports and exports has shifted, under the pressures of a rising exchange rate, with the emergence of an adverse balance in manufactures from 1983 – though the depreciation of the pound during 1986 led to an upsurge in manufacturing output in 1987, when it rose by 5.7%. Britain has been a significant oil exporter in global markets during the 1980s. For several years it has, for example, been one of the three leading suppliers to the German market, alongside Saudi Arabia and Iran. The UK share of world markets in technology-intensive products has continued to decline in the 1980s, from 12% in 1965 to 10.8% in 1980 and 8.5% in 1984, behind the United States, Japan and Germany, and narrowly ahead of France.[7] Whether Britain's relative weakness in high-technology sectors outside pharmaceuticals and chemicals, or its broader relative weakness in overall trade in manufactures, are matters with which governments should be actively concerned is the subject of much controversy within British politics, and we shall return to it below.

The changing economic environment

The international environment in which the British economy operates has changed rapidly and radically over the past twenty-five years, and will change as radically between the late 1980s and 2010. The British economy has grown more open to international markets, as successive GATT rounds have liberalized trade, as air transport and electronic communications have cut time-lags in international transactions, and as privatization and deregulation have lowered the barriers erected by previous governments. The broadening flow of inward and outward investment has made the economy less 'British', while extending the reach of successful British companies to a global scale.

Most industrial production in the 1950s was on a national scale, with a small proportion of components brought in from overseas. The integration of industrial production, with components from around the world assembled into products designed and developed centrally for the global market, has progressed enormously since then – allowing General Motors to switch final assembly between plants in Britain and 'Germany in response to changing exchange rates and productivity levels, and making Ford one of Britain's top ten exporters *and* importers. One quarter of Britain's external trade now consists of 'captive' trade flows, carried on between affiliates of the same parent company in fields such as electronics, aerospace, chemicals, and even textiles (through outward processing). In 1987 30% of manufactured production in Britain was sold overseas, while 35% of British demand for manufactured products was met by imports.

There are fewer and fewer industrial sectors for which the British market is now the appropriate frame of reference: to talk about a 'national' economy is thus in some ways an anachronism. 'There is no longer any such thing as a purely domestic policy,' Sir Geoffrey Howe remarked in Tokyo in January 1988. 'Open economies are interdependent, and have to be outward-looking.'[8] The integration of international financial markets has moved further and faster than that of industrial markets, though national regulation, giving way only slowly to pressures for international deregulation, has so far inhibited the integration of financial, as compared with industrial, institutions.

The balance of the international economy has also shifted significantly. The global economy in the early 1960s was transatlantic, reflecting the recovery of Western Europe, which was spurred on by American economic aid, an open US market, and extensive investment in Europe by US multinational companies. The global economy of the late 1980s is as much trans-Pacific as transatlantic, thanks to the remarkable growth of the Asian newly industrializing countries – dependent in their turn upon access to an open US market, and assisted not only by the investment of US companies but also by Japanese example, investment and technology. This East Asian and trans-Pacific orientation is likely to become still more marked over the next decade, as Malaysia,

Thailand, the Philippines and perhaps Indonesia begin to follow the path taken by South Korea, Taiwan, Hong Kong and Singapore, and as (and if) the Chinese economy opens to its neighbours.

At the same time, other centres of industrial and financial strength are developing. Some Middle East oil producers have already accumulated substantial overseas assets; the Kuwait Investment Office, for example, is an important (and sometimes controversial) actor in the investment markets of Britain, Federal Germany and Spain. The probable decline of non-Opec oil production in the course of the 1990s will leave the Gulf countries once again in a strong position in terms both of financial assets and of energy markets. Despite the overhang of international debt (and behind a particularly protectionist regime) Brazil is developing an impressive industrial base, extending into such advanced sectors as aerospace and biotechnology. The pattern of global trade is itself changing, with traditional heavy manufactures giving way to the more valuable and technology-intensive lightweight goods, with the integration of ownership and production across national boundaries eroding the old distinctions between trade and capital flows, and with information itself becoming one of the most valued and rapidly moving commodities.

However successful the British economy is over the next ten years in sustaining a growth rate higher than those of its immediate neighbours, it is unlikely to avoid some further deterioration in its position in the world economy. Barring political upheaval, the potential for growth of the industrializing economies of East and South Asia is inescapably higher than that of the mature industrialized economies of the OECD countries, and it is reinforced by the high rates of domestic saving and the heavy investment in education and technological skills which many of these countries are now achieving. Over the past quarter-century economic power has shifted away from the United States – the dominant player in shaping and enforcing the rules of international economic cooperation, as well as the provider of the world's reserve currency – to the loose grouping of governments represented in the G-7 economic summits and, more broadly, to other OECD countries.

Unless there is a breakdown in international economic order, the prospect for the next quarter-century is of a further dispersion of economic power, across Asia and – perhaps – across some parts of

Latin America. Sustained British economic growth in the face of such competition may serve to regain some of the ground lost over the past three decades in relation to France, the Federal Republic, Italy and the Netherlands. But that relative achievement may well be placed within the context of a West European economy substantially outperformed by the newly industrializing countries. Britain has long ceased to be at the centre of world trade. In the international economy of the twenty-first century it could become an offshore financial centre to a regional economy of secondary importance if the dynamism of Asian growth and competitiveness is sustained.

Collective management in an integrated world economy
According to the logic of a liberal economic order and a commitment to free trade, the question of where Britain's interests lie in the future development of the global economy might be considered irrelevant. Governments, it may be argued, best serve the interests of their citizens by opening their economies to the competitive forces of the international market; if other governments refuse to follow their example, they will succeed only in damaging their long-term interests in the attempt to protect particular producers. Free trade as an ideology is internationalist, and deliberately subversive of nationalism, national power and national sovereignty – the central concerns of mercantilists. 'The interests of states', a *Financial Times* leader-writer recently commented, 'are not necessarily those of their citizens. "Japan", "Germany" and the "UK" are powerful but dangerous abstract ideas, capable of evoking calamitous loyalties and hatreds ... The principal achievement of Adam Smith's economics may be the proposition that the raison d'être of economic activity is consumption of individuals, of which they themselves are normally the best judge.'[9]

The integration of national markets – of production, finance, ownership, consumer preferences – into broader regional and global markets has made it more difficult for any national government to define where its 'national interests' lie. The growth of multinational companies in the postwar years led Charles Kindleberger to conclude, twenty years ago, that 'the state is about through as an economic unit.'[10] The boundaries between domestic economies have eroded much further since then. The definition of a 'British' company is no longer an easy task: should IBM, for example, with a well-established presence, including research facilities, in Britain and

throughout Western Europe, be considered less British than
Amstrad, which has its controlling board and headquarters in
Britain but subcontracts substantial areas of production to foreign-
owned companies and depends heavily on components from
abroad? The idea of national identity becomes blurred when the
interpenetration of economies, ownership and employment
advances beyond a certain point. Even the concept of an
independent currency as a fundamental attribute of sovereignty is
tightly constrained when the Bank of England is caught up in hour-
by-hour cooperation with other central banks in managing the
exchanges, in working to stabilize rapidly moving markets, and in
consulting on and concerting interest-rate changes across the major
financial capitals of the world.

Yet the international economy is by no means an entirely
integrated and self-balancing market, over which the actions of
individual governments can and should have marginal effects. The
maintenance of a liberal economic order depends upon the
acceptance – and, if necessary, the enforcement – of rules governing
the interaction of private and public actors, enabling them to
transact business with a sufficient degree of confidence in the
continuation of the regime within which they operate. Governments
establish the framework and enforce the rules in national economies.
The United States in effect played this role within the postwar
international economy, until the growth of other industrialized
economies undermined its hegemonic position. The inability of the
United States and its major partners to agree on a common strategy
for collective economic management led during the 1970s to a
partial retreat from the open and stable international economic
order to which the major countries were in principle committed, first
through the abandonment of the fixed-exchange-rate system, and
more gradually through the re-emergence of protectionist barriers:
the quotas, voluntary export restraints and other administrative
measures of the 'new' protectionism. The evidence of the 1970s and
early 1980s, Richard Cooper has concluded, is that 'it does not seem
possible to assure stability for decentralized policy-making': without
active collective economic management, the international economy
exhibits slow growth, financial instability, and rising conflict over
national economic advantage.[11] The United Kingdom, as one of the
world's most open economies, has a particularly strong interest in
promoting the effective management of international economic

relations through collaboration among national governments.

International economic collaboration is a profoundly political process, in which the participating governments bargain to structure the rules of cooperation to their own advantage. The absence of a central authority makes the provision of collective goods – such as economic assistance, international credit, willingness to expand domestic demand when international recession threatens – a matter of intergovernmental bargaining. There is a persistent 'free rider' problem, with second-order countries attempting to take advantage of the obligations and rules which others accept without observing them themselves – through aggressive export-promotion strategies, the manipulation of exchange rates, even counterfeiting. There is an unavoidable degree of linkage between the provision of security and the political management of the international economy; the United States has repeatedly reminded its allies of this, most vividly in the sharp-tempered exchanges of the 'Year of Europe' in 1973. The G-7 summits have added political and security issues to their original economic agenda, implicitly accepting Henry Kissinger's repeated insistence on 'the crucial relationship between economic vitality and global stability'.[12]

The rhetoric of free trade and the reality of intergovernmental bargaining have made for a certain ambivalence in the British government's approach to international economic policy. There is, after all, a structural contradiction between the logic of international industrial and economic integration and the national framework of popular loyalty and legitimacy. The emphasis which the government has placed upon economic strength as the basis for a more vigorous foreign policy sits uneasily with the emphasis it also places upon taking the state out of the economy, in international as well as in domestic transactions. If the central role of government in foreign policy is seen as the maintenance of the integrity of national boundaries and the protection of national interests – as it traditionally has been in British foreign policy – then an unqualified commitment to free trade amounts, by comparison, to unilateral disarmament (which is why theory and practice sometimes diverge).

The policy agenda
The most difficult issues on the agenda of international economic policy result from the clash between the incompatible objectives of

national independence and a liberal economic order. They include the appropriate governmental response to the progressive integration of markets and economies, as national regulations and patterns of market management are outdated and outflanked. Domestic deregulation, intergovernmental bargaining on mutual liberalization, and negotiation on international regimes for regulation may all form part of that response. Collective management – of international financial markets first and foremost, but also of macroeconomic policies and of disputes over the rules of international trade – has become an increasingly important aspect, with governments bargaining with each other to achieve what none can obtain alone. Alongside these there remains the difficult question of the use of state power and resources to promote the competitiveness of the national economy, through actions intended to tilt the balance of international markets in a favourable direction and to improve domestic capabilities for meeting international competition. These actions range from investment in education, research and development to the use of public procurement policies and other 'industrial' strategies, including for many governments the subsidies and non-tariff barriers of the new protectionism.

The dilemmas presented are not unique to Britain. The contradictions of West German policy – preaching the virtues of open markets, while practising extensive industrial and agricultural subsidies, and maintaining substantial barriers against foreign competition in services – are readily apparent. The Gaullist alternative in France presented a determined resistance to the multinational drift, using all the instruments available to a well-organized central government to negotiate the terms of interdependence, issue by issue, so as to retain as much autonomy as possible within the limits set by international competition. No British government over the past thirty years has handled the dilemmas posed with great success. What makes the problems more acute for the present government, however, is the more explicit emphasis it places *both* on national autonomy *and* on international markets. The frequency of changes in the structure of the Department of Trade and Industry (DTI), and in its ministerial heads, bears ample witness to the consequent uncertainties of policy.

The government's implicit strategy for resolving the dilemmas has been to attempt to extend liberalization and deregulation from domestic to international markets, through example, exhortation and negotiation. The confidence with which the Prime Minister speaks of foreign 'imitation' of Britain's example rests heavily upon the extent to which other governments, with varying degrees of enthusiasm and success, have followed the example of British deregulatory and privatizing policies. British support for American efforts to use the GATT Uruguay round to maintain the momentum of liberalization by carrying deregulation into the service sector represents a parallel effort – through negotiation – on the global level. But the central element in Britain's strategy from the mid-1980s was on the European level, with British ministers enthusiastically supporting the Community's objective of a single internal market by the end of 1992.

This mixture of unilateral and multilateral measures, of national deregulation and intergovernmental bargaining on reciprocal liberalization, rests upon the assumption that the weight of national economic policies throughout the industrialized world can be shifted away from intervention and protection towards economic liberalism. 'The emergence of the new protectionism in the Western world' in the 1970s reflected 'the victory of the interventionist, or welfare, economy over the market economy.'[13] The reversal of that trend during the 1980s depended heavily upon the political commitment of the Reagan administration: the success of British policy, here again, depended upon the support of the United States. Federal Germany, concerned to defend the social dimension of its social market economic policies, has been a much more reluctant partner – even, on some issues, an opponent. Japanese governments have been as reluctant, leading Mrs Thatcher and other British ministers to stress the principle of reciprocity in attempting to open the Japanese financial sector – for example – to British participants.

The British government is, in effect, engaged in a gigantic gamble, leading the world in the dismantling of national barriers and of the instruments of industrial and technological support. If the rest of the world continues to follow – most crucially, the United States, under a new president and a changing Congress – the British economy will benefit from its early adaptation to open global competition. If current trends are reversed, however, British ministers may be faced with some painful choices between continued openness, the pursuit of a regional open market within the European Community, and a return to more isolated national policies. It is not surprising, therefore, that the principle of reciprocity is now being invoked by

Britain in its dealings with other countries, notably Japan.

The increasing importance of the West European dimension for Britain's economy now means that policy must be made with reference to three interlinked arenas: the national, the European and the global. British monetary policy, for example, has become a delicate game of balancing between these three. Domestic interest rates, the sterling/Deutschmark exchange rate and the sterling/ dollar exchange rate present ministers with policy preferences which are often difficult to reconcile. The shift in Britain's external trade patterns over the past twenty years has made the sterling/D-mark rate more central to Britain's international competitiveness than the value of sterling against the dollar – the traditional focus. Shifts in the policies of other European governments (partly in response to the implications of the 1992 target for the creation of the 'single European market', for which the British government itself has pressed) may in the medium-term future present policy-makers with yet more difficult choices.

Refusal to link the pound formally to the D-mark and the other major European currencies through the exchange-rate mechanisms of the EMS rests partly upon prime ministerial determination to maintain the autonomy of British economic policy, and partly – implicitly – upon a traditional association between sovereignty and an independent national currency. Moves towards the development of a more integrated system of monetary cooperation, including extended use of the ECU and plans for the creation of a European central bank, will be shaped by those who are the most active players in the current system. British ministers may again decide to accept exclusion from the central bargaining process, as the Labour chancellor and Treasury officials accepted exclusion from Franco-German discussions on the EMS proposal (which had begun on a trilateral basis) in 1978.[14] But as with the EMS proposals, the outcome of such a reticent approach is likely to be the creation of a new framework for collaborative policy which suits the needs of other governments more than those of Britain, rather than an effective British veto which prevents the proposals from going ahead.

Coordination of global economic policies among the trilateral partners of Japan, Europe and the United States presents the British government with similar short- and long-term dilemmas. The dominant players in attempts at international economic management, from the 1978 Bonn seven-power-summit package through to the 1985 Plaza Agreement and the 1987 Louvre Accord, have been the United States, Japan and Federal Germany: the world's three most powerful economies and three key currencies. The dominant players in international economic bargaining in the 1990s will be the United States and Japan – with the European Community as the third actor if current proposals for further economic and monetary integration are carried through. British interests across the range of current international economic negotiations are closer in some instances to those of the US administration, in others to those of its West European partners. But the dynamics of West European political and economic integration *and* of global negotiations are likely to force British representatives to exert their influence through the medium of a West European 'caucus', bargaining – in some cases on the basis of formal Community positions, in others on the basis of informal intergovernmental agreements – with the US and Japan.

Such policy bargaining will need to reach further and further into areas of domestic economic policy – fiscal and budgetary, as well as monetary – which have until now been entirely matters of national discretion, if a stable, prosperous and ever-more integrated economic order is to be maintained. From the perspective of economic policy, Richard Cooper has argued, what is required among the major industrialized countries is no less than the coordination of national economic policies and policy instruments within the framework of agreed collective goals.

> Decision-making at the supranational level, or its analytical near-equivalent, continuous international coordination of national policy actions, can always in principle lead to results that are superior to those produced by rule-based regimes . . . but they do so only by threatening existing decision-making arrangements at the national level, and constitutional change at the national level entails costs as well.[15]

If this is the case at the global level, the conflict between economic requirements and political constraints is even sharper at the regional – European Community – level, which provides the most highly structured framework for the coordination of British policies with those of other governments. The strength of feeling aroused both in government and in Parliament by Lord Cockfield's proposals for approximation of European VAT and excise tax rates, on grounds of economic sovereignty as much as on detailed objections to the proposals as presented, indicates the extent of the problem.

Neither the disengagement of government from the management of industry and the domestic economy, nor the internationalization of business and finance, have yet removed from government, or from the public, a sense of national economic interests to be promoted, or of national economic security to be protected. The Prime Minister has herself devoted increasing time and attention in recent years to supporting British companies in the pursuit of major overseas contracts, and to exerting pressure on foreign governments and companies to accommodate themselves to Britain's perceived interests.

She personally interviewed the chairman of Nissan in Tokyo in September 1982 over his company's investment intentions in Britain and over the terms and conditions on which it would commit itself to car manufacture within the British market. In 1988 she raised with the Japanese prime minister the issue of a seat on the Tokyo stock exchange for a particular British firm. She unsuccessfully lobbied President Reagan in a transatlantic telephone call on the US army's choice between British (Ptarmigan) and French (Rita) field radar systems in 1985, bringing arguments about political and security relations, as well as commercial and technological considerations, to bear. She vigorously recommended British nuclear submarines to the Canadian Parliament in the middle of a formal speech immediately after the 1988 Toronto summit; while at the summit itself she had intervened with the President of the European Commission, M. Delors, over the application of EC rules to the takeover of Austin Rover by British Aerospace.

British trade ministers freely use the language of mercantilism, insisting that the 'negotiation of trading agreements involves hardheaded bargaining of reciprocal advantage and concessions', that 'one thing we are not prepared to do is unilaterally disarm; multilateral disarmament is what we are working towards.'[16] Michael Heseltine, from the Conservative back benches, has argued for a more explicitly mercantilist approach, against what he calls 'the imperial and Treasury nexus', with its assumption that British financial and industrial interests are identical and that both are best promoted through free trade. 'Without industry and government in partnership', he urged some months after his resignation over the sale of Westland helicopters to an American company, 'you will be sunk in the modern world. Economies are in the business of winning. There's no-one else in the world playing a different game.'[17]

Sir Michael Edwardes, in his contribution to the Board of Trade Bicentenary Lectures in 1986, set out an agenda for government in seeking to establish 'a clear view of what is needed for international success ... I refer to such issues as: what makes for competitive economies of scale; the need for collaboration; the need to see the world scene and not to fall back on Little England as a solution; the need for fair rather than naively free trade policies; and above all, the right climate for enterprise.' This, in his view, required from government 'a clear-cut Cabinet-endorsed approach to industry and to commerce [such] as there is in Japan and Germany and, by implication, in the United States'.[18]

Questions of government intervention versus non-intervention, of reciprocity versus unilateral deregulation, of the appropriateness of the national framework for policy versus the European or the global framework, are repeatedly and unavoidably raised as specific issues arise. The widening flow of inward and outward investment, for example, raises awkward questions about preferred foreign partners, about competition policy, and about whether British ownership is a significant value to be promoted in adjusting to international economic integration. In the financial sector the government has attempted to set clear limits to British dependence on foreign centres of decision-making. 'It is of the highest importance', the Governor of the Bank of England stated in October 1987, 'that there should be a strong and continuing British presence in the banking system of the United Kingdom. It runs counter to common sense to argue that the openness of the London market must be carried to the point where control of the core of our financial system – the payments mechanism, the supply of credit – may pass into the hands of institutions whose business aims and national interest lie elsewhere.'[19]

In the industrial sector government policy remains less clear and subject to political controversy – as shown by the Westland affair, by the proposed sale of parts of British Leyland (BL) to Ford and General Motors, and by the competing bids for British Caledonian from British Airways and SAS. David Hart's passionate plea in the BL case that a government which believes in the free market 'should sell to the highest bidder, British or American' was answered by *The Financial Times*'s careful conclusion that 'there is a difference in

The economic dimension

character between a British-owned business, with its top management and key research and engineering facilities located in the UK, and the subsidiary of a foreign company; ideally there should be a balance between the two sorts of enterprise.'[20] Privatization – of British Telecom, of BP, where the sale of the British government's 30% holding led to the Kuwait Investment Office accumulating 22% – has made the dilemmas which face governments more acute. They may prove particularly acute in the communications sector, as global television networks and newspaper companies develop, with the regulatory policies of *other* governments – most of all the US government – shaping the strategies of multinational companies.

In 1986 the government intervened to prevent a proposed merger between GEC and Plessey, in response to representations from the Ministry of Defence (MoD) that the resulting company would dominate the *British* market. The DTI's policy document on competition policy, published after an eighteen-month review in February 1988, still took the national framework as given. 'Merger issues', *The Financial Times* protested, 'are discussed as though the UK's membership of the European Community were a technicality ... A fuller discussion of the issues raised by European integration would have been timely.'[21] Barely two months later the Nestlé bid for Rowntree, in deliberate pursuit of an integrated strategy for the European market, led to widespread demands for a reconsideration of policy criteria on takeovers and mergers.

Despite considerable reductions in support for industry and for high-technology research and development, the British government retains an active involvement in this field. This is partly due to the MoD's role as the dominant purchaser of military high technology. The MoD is the largest single customer for the products of British industry. 'Defence procurement supports some 350,000 jobs in the United Kingdom', the 1988 *Statement on the Defence Estimates* noted, 'and thus plays an important role in economic and industrial activity.'[22] The politics of international collaboration in military procurement require governments to bargain hard for industrial advantage, as well as for preferred military requirements, according to the principle of *juste retour*.

In civil high technology the definition of the national interest is less well established, and the extent to which British governments should be involved has become a matter of political controversy. The same sceptical approach which the government has shown to

52

the rationale for such international 'obligations' as membership of UNESCO has been applied to the network of European collaboration in high technology which has grown up over the past twenty-four years. A reduced British presence in the European Space Agency, insistence that the EUREKA initiative should not involve any additional public expenditure, resistance to CERN's expenditure plans, all such measures have reduced the burden of support for international technology on the British budget. But the effect of a less active and interventionist British policy has been to leave decisions on civil high-technology development not to the interplay of private actors in the international market, but to other governments working alongside their favoured companies – above all, the effect has been a developing pattern of European collaboration shaped by the governments of France and Federal Germany, in competition with explicit or implicit government/industry partnerships in the USA and Japan.

Two interrelated questions arise about the appropriate role for government in international competition in high technology. The first concerns the nature of the international market, and the extent to which the evolution of industrial location and control is now shaped by market forces. As Robert Gilpin has noted:

> Every advanced economy has witnessed the partial displacement
> of competitive markets composed of many small firms by
> imperfect markets in which immense concentrations of corpor-
> ate power exist. With the decline of trade barriers and increas-
> ing economic interdependence, a similar phenomenon has
> appeared at the level of the international economy.

This in itself need not be of direct concern to British policy-makers, unless they also accept Professor Gilpin's argument that in this process 'global trading patterns, the distribution of economic benefits, and the national location of production have been affected to an indeterminate extent by strategic interactions among oligopolistic firms and national governments.'[23]

Some American economists would go further, arguing that in advanced industrial sectors 'the pattern of trade specialisation may be arbitrary, and factors such as noncompetitive firm behaviour and government intervention may determine which country prevails.'[24] The image of a global economy in which multinational companies operate from home markets which give them a degree of entrenched advantage in global competition, with the support of governments prepared to invest heavily in education, training, and long-term research, is a long way from the model of the open international market depicted by orthodox Western economists. It conjures up a world in which the shifting balance of international power is determined more by the drive for economic advantage than by the possession of military forces, a mercantilist world, with bargaining among economic blocs about the rules under which companies may gain access to technology and markets – a world in which the Japanese example is accepted as the model, rather than the British.[25]

The second question concerns the relationship between military and civil technology, and the problem of 'strategic dependence' on other countries for key technologies. This issue has been on the British government's agenda since the late 1950s. Macmillan's Cabinet set the pattern by turning first to the United States to supply the technological needs which Britain could not fulfil on its own, and then also initiating collaboration with other West European governments. As Mrs Thatcher's government has discovered in its turn, it is most often cost-effective in each specific instance to buy military equipment (and civil aircraft) from the United States, rather than to attempt to develop 'national' alternatives or to invest in European collaboration. But long-term questions of technological dependency (itself a contested term), of the impact of an accumulation of such decisions on Britain's industrial base, and of the political conditions which might be imposed upon future supply, all throw doubt upon the wisdom of such an alternative.

Experience of US restrictions on technological transfer, as used under the Reagan administration, have not been reassuring, and have pushed the British government into erecting legal defences against the invasion of British sovereignty by American claims to extra-territorial jurisdiction.[26] In the mid-1980s the MoD and the DTI appear at times to have been pursuing conflicting policies in the overlapping spheres of civil and military high technology – most evident perhaps in government policy towards the exploitation of space, where MoD confidence in continued access to American systems cut across the DTI's determinedly civil approach to British participation in European space collaboration. In the long run, a recent Chatham House Paper argued, Britain will have either to accept that it is a user under licence of space technologies produced by others, or to pursue a more coherent collaborative policy, in which it will be 'increasingly difficult to avoid making a choice between the current mix of European and transatlantic connections and a more European orientation'.[27]

A British government might choose to leave the leading edge of advanced technology to others, judging the public expenditure they commit to long-term projects ill-considered and the benefits in second-guessing future market needs intangible. It might similarly allow the presence or absence of strong British-based companies in international markets, and the strength or weakness of Britain's industrial base, to emerge out of the cut and thrust of individual company strategies and the interventions – ill-judged or intelligent – of other governments. There are respectable economic arguments for following such a course, though the dilemmas of assessing competition policy and policy on mergers within the overlapping contexts of national, European and global markets would make it difficult to follow that course consistently.

We doubt, however, if such a course is consistent with the reassertion of self-confidence and pride which is at the heart of Mrs Thatcher's foreign policy. A country's prestige and standing abroad are partly dependent upon the image others have of its industrial and technological competence – a factor strongly evident in French policy, and present also in the policies of the USA, the USSR, West Germany and Japan. A country without a strong research base will lose its best and brightest intellectuals, as happens already in some of the smaller European countries. A country without a strong domestic presence in the ownership of finance, service companies *and* industry will suffer an erosion of talent and of autonomy which will in time sap its self-confidence. It is likely also over time to sap its economic prosperity, as decisions taken elsewhere serve other national interests rather than its own.

The costs of foreign policy

The burden of international responsibilities on Britain's economy has been a recurrent preoccupation for successive governments since the end of World War II. Conversely, the inadequacy of the resources available to pursue foreign policy objectives has been a painful constraint on every prime minister and foreign secretary since Attlee and Bevin. Harold Macmillan, as Chancellor of the Exchequer in May 1956, dared to muse in public about the transformation of

Britain's economic position and balance of payments which could be achieved by the 'pipe dream' of a 50% cut in Britain's defence budget. Britain, he argued, was shouldering far more than its 'fair share' of the common burden of maintaining international order, though he concluded that 'by and large Britain will have to go on carrying two rifles rather than the one carried by others.'[28] Sir Paul Gore-Booth (later Lord Gore-Booth) proposed a further study of the fundamental problem of the effect of 'the chronic and, as far as one can see, enduring if not increasing "international poverty" of the United Kingdom on our foreign policy generally' in the aftermath of the 1957 Defence Review, raising the question of whether Britain should continue to see itself 'as a world power or as a busy little island engaged in trade and manufacture but relying on others to preserve its political interests'.[29] Sir Nicholas Henderson's 1979 'farewell despatch' echoed the same theme, though without suggesting so heretically that sharp reductions in Britain's spending on defence and foreign policy would help to reverse the pattern of economic decline.

Britain has seen itself as a responsible actor on the international stage for the past forty years, accepting as one of its underlying foreign policy objectives 'to honour certain commitments or obligations which the UK has voluntarily entered into or cannot withdraw from'.[30] With successive postwar cuts in information and cultural expenditure, and with an aid budget below the OECD's average over the past ten years, that responsibility has been shouldered overwhelmingly in the defence budget. Financial difficulties enforced a reluctant withdrawal from Britain's East of Suez commitment twenty years ago. But Britain's contribution to the common defence remains close, in absolute terms, to those of France and Germany, and therefore higher in per capita terms than that of any other Nato member except the United States and Greece. (It is now at 4.7%, against 4.0% for France and 3.0% for Federal Germany, according to the statistics of the 1988 Defence White Paper; its drop from the 5–5.2% at which it had hovered for several years reflects both the welcome growth in the British economy and a shift of policy in containing defence expenditure 'at current levels'.) Italy, with an economy roughly the same size as Britain's, spends half as much on defence.

The rationale for Britain's present defence posture, and the threats against which it protects itself, are considered further in the following chapter. Here we merely wish to pose the question of the appropriate level of Britain's contribution to the international public goods of security, order and economic development. As Paul Kennedy and others have argued, there is a natural tendency for responsibilities and commitments to linger on beyond periods of imperial hegemony, to weigh down the economies of nations in political decline.[31] We note the current debate within Japan on the appropriate level and distribution of contributions that its healthy economy should now be making to the international order as a whole.[32] We also note the widespread belief within Japan that its low level of defence spending was a contributory factor in the country's rapid economic growth, and that 'excessive' defence spending has weighed down both the American and British economies. We recognize the strong likelihood that efforts to bring under control America's twin trade and budget deficits will involve a progressive reduction in the US contribution to world economic development and to the defence of Western security interests.

Pressures on West European countries to shoulder a greater share of the burden of Western security are already strong, and will grow stronger. Pressures from Third World countries, who want to reduce their dependence on the United States by turning to the European Community and its member countries for a larger proportion of the development assistance they need, are also mounting, especially in North Africa, Central America and the Caribbean countries. The British government will be faced with a succession of awkward choices as it responds; these relate not only to the immediate budgetary costs of the obligations proposed, but to Britain's image of itself as an international actor on a level with the more prosperous economies of the USA, West Germany, Japan and France.

A particular set of questions arise within the field of international expenditure about the appropriate objectives and level of Britain's aid budget. Britain's overseas aid programme evolved historically out of its imperial obligations to colonial development. The shift of American policy, and UN concern, at the end of the 1950s from assisting postwar economic recovery to promoting global economic development added a broader multilateral dimension to Britain's bilateral arrangements, to which the UK government became a major donor. Historical and cultural obligations remain in British assistance to the anglophone Caribbean, to southern African countries, and to the Commonwealth micro-states of the Pacific. But the number of cases for which Britain should now feel obliged to bear the main burden is very small.

As the French government drew West German resources in to assist the development of francophone Africa through the creation of the European Development Fund, so British policy should be concerned to draw in Japanese – as well as Continental – resources to share the burden of supporting development in southern Africa and elsewhere. The British government has a particular interest in the management of the immense overhang of Third World debts, given the involvement of London-based banks; but this is above all a shared problem of international economic instability, to which the structural-surplus countries should appropriately make the largest contribution. British policy, here as with many other international economic issues, is better directed towards multilateral cooperation in addressing common problems than towards independent actions seen to be serving specifically British interests.

There are, of course, other political and commercial objectives at stake in aid expenditure, which merit a continuing bilateral programme. British capital exports to the Third World depend for competitiveness in financial arrangements partly upon the subsidy aspects of the Aid and Trade Provision, competing against the often more generous financial packages provided by other governments. But this is a matter rather more of how far it is felt appropriate for the British government to act in support of British industry in international markets than of aid policy as such. Interest-rate subsidies for exports through the Export Credit Guarantee Department provide a similar form of financial support, and as such have been a focus not only for domestic controversy, but also for successive intergovernmental negotiations on competitive subsidies.

The increasing interpenetration of Britain's domestic society and economy with their counterparts in other countries is lowering the traditional boundaries between domestic public expenditure and the costs of foreign policy. As more and more domestic ministries are drawn into intergovernmental business, so international commitments are becoming part of the battle between Whitehall's spending departments and the Treasury – with the Treasury's role in controlling public expenditure making it a significant player across the spreading field of international policies. This is not just a matter of joint military procurement, or Nato commitments on national levels of defence spending, or the European Community budget – though these account for the most costly single items. Negotiations on international standards for power station emissions, or reductions in coastal pollution, carry direct implications for domestic public expenditure, as much as collaborative programmes in meteorological research or nuclear fusion. 'Overseas aspects of public expenditure will become increasingly important as the British economy becomes relatively smaller and more open to the world economy,' the Treasury's Deputy Chief Economic Adviser has remarked.[33]

Britain's autonomy in setting the terms of domestic public expenditure is thus constrained by the behaviour of other governments and by the obligations arising from multilateral bargaining over the conditions of international cooperation and competition. Efforts to reduce public expenditure come up against continuing pressures for government intervention, and government financial support, in the pursuit of long-term industrial and technological priorities in fiercely competitive world markets. The priorities of public expenditure in support of British foreign policy objectives have, however, been directed to military, rather than to civil, ends more emphatically than those of any of Britain's industrialized partners and competitors except the United States.

5
THE SECURITY DIMENSION

National security covers a much broader area than is implied by the way in which the term is habitually used within the British political debate, where it is confined to discussion of military threats and the protection of government secrets. There are more general threats to British security than the power and ideology of the Soviet Union, or the publication of information about Britain's security services. The external challenges that Britain faces are as much political, economic and industrial as military, arising from an international environment over which Britain's influence has progressively declined since the highpoint of its power in the late nineteenth century.

It is – as we noted in the preceding chapter – a matter of some controversy in Britain how far it is an appropriate sphere for state action to guard against such threats. Japanese governments since World War II have seen as one of their primary tasks the creation of a strong and independent national economy, which would avoid the vulnerability of dependence on potentially hostile dominant suppliers for key raw materials, manufactures or commodities.[1] French governments have similarly been concerned to manage the awkward trade-off between sovereignty and interdependence, seeking to use state power to further French interests, to limit their economic and industrial dependence on the United States and to bargain with their partners on the terms of cooperation. They have also been actively concerned with perceived threats to cultural autonomy, and thus to the nation itself – a preoccupation which Canadian governments, and to some extent also German governments, have shared. The American administration has, since the launch of the first Soviet sputnik in 1957, included the quality and spread of national education, research and training within its definition of national security, providing extensive funds – through the National Defense Education Act and other channels – for scientific research and studies of the Soviet Union, China and elsewhere.

The British approach has been distinctive in its concentration on the military aspects of security, and in its ambivalence about considerations of economic autonomy, industry or culture. This ambivalence also extends to the use of economic or cultural resources in the furtherance of foreign policy objectives and in the maintenance of national security. Commitment to continuing British sovereignty in terms of military power, symbolized by the development and modernization of an independent nuclear deterrent, has coexisted with official resistance to mercantilist national policies outside the military domain. Of course, the projection of military power serves broader foreign policy purposes than that of national defence, pure and simple: it adds to its possessor's weight in international diplomacy, giving it greater access to and influence in the capitals of friendly and of hostile powers alike. But the utility of military power to its possessors, both in the achievement and in the maintenance of international stature, appears to be in decline. The Soviet Union has discovered the limitations of military strength without economic or political weight, and has conducted an internal debate about the role of military and non-military factors in the 'correlation of forces'. Japan has reacquired the status of a first-rank power without abandoning the constitutional and budgetary restraints on its self-defence forces.

But in Britain the security issue has been defined primarily in terms of the military dimension. Defence policy has evolved out of the interaction of a number of underlying considerations: first, the nature of the military threats which Britain faces; second, the broader foreign policy objectives which British military power is seen to serve; third, the accumulated commitments which successive governments have accepted, the limitations imposed by equipment and forces already in place, and the costs the government is prepared to shoulder in providing forces and equipment for the foreseeable future to meet its commitments.

The security dimension

The nature of the threat
In 1940–41 the United Kingdom faced the real and immediate threat
of hostile invasion, and faced it virtually alone: it was the ultimate
threat to national security, requiring the mobilization of the nation's
full resources to resist. The threat from the Soviet Union which
rapidly succeeded the defeat of Germany was seen in military terms
as not much less direct. With Germany disarmed and continental
Western Europe struggling to rebuild its shattered economies, it was
feared that a determined Soviet drive could have reached the
Channel within a short space of time. The Soviet Union was seen as
a direct threat to the survival of the British state and of British
values in a much broader sense. Internal subversion, within Britain
as well as within Britain's Continental neighbours, might powerfully
assist the Soviet Union's revolutionary-expansionist aims. In the
postwar years the work of the security services was considered to be
as essential as the re-equipment of Britain's military forces in
combating what was perceived to be the clear and immediate danger
presented by Soviet power.

The core military threat to Britain has been seen for centuries as the
achievement by a single state of domination on the European
continent. From the late seventeenth century until 1815 that threat
was posed by France. Its elimination allowed Britain to concentrate
its energies and its military forces on extra-European imperial responsibilities for most of the next century, until the threat of German
domination became acute. After two major wars, which had dragged
Britain, along with its American and imperial allies, into redressing
the imbalance of the European continent, the Continent was itself
divided between two hostile coalitions. The initiators of the European
Community set out to counter the threat of a revived, though
truncated, West Germany, and to overcome the hostility between
Germany and its neighbours, through containing the new Federal
Republic within a broader West European framework. They saw
Britain from the outset as a necessary factor, alongside France, in
counterbalancing German power. The categorical WEU commitment of British forces to Germany was an essential requirement for
the French government before it accepted the necessity of German
rearmament. British, French and American forces in Germany were
there to keep Germany's national forces in check, and thus to
forestall the re-emergence of a potential threat from Germany, as
well as to protect against the more immediate Soviet threat. As a

saying popular in the British services put it, Nato was created 'to keep the Americans in, the Germans down, and the Russians out'.

The threats which Britain will face in the 1990s will be more diffuse. There is no immediate or plausible threat to the integrity of the United Kingdom alone. The threat posed by Germany has now followed that posed by France into the history books, dissolved within the developing community of Western Europe well before those British citizens who will be reaching adulthood in the 1990s were born. The Soviet threat as it is now presented is to Western Europe as a whole, most specifically to West Germany.

The position of Germany and the nature of its relations with its neighbours remains for both sides – now, as at the end of World War II – the key to the future of European security. The threat to Britain is thus part of a shared threat to which some of our West European allies are even more acutely vulnerable. It has to be met through concerted military efforts, in which the British government accepts that 'the forward defence of the Federal Republic is the forward defence of Britain itself.'[2]

The Soviet threat to Western Europe is also becoming less direct, and perhaps also less real. 'There is no reason to believe that Soviet leaders want war in Europe,' the 1988 Defence White Paper declared. 'Although it would be imprudent to rely on a sustained change in Soviet attitudes, the prospect of its taking place is a challenge that the West must accept.'[3] The image of a strong and inherently expansionist Soviet Union has been undermined by the growing evidence of Soviet economic and political weakness. As Zbigniev Brezinski recently told the Centre for Policy Studies, 'the Soviet empire is clearly on the defensive.'

> This has far-reaching implications. It means that in a significant way the competition for the future of Europe, which has been under way for some 40 years now, is shifting from the political defence of Western Europe against possible Soviet domination to the problem of the survival of Soviet domination in the East. It is a geopolitical and historical shift of some importance.[4]

It is also a shift which poses some awkward problems for Britain and for its Western allies. 'The Soviet threat has been a kind of solution for many of us for a long time,' Michael Howard has remarked. 'What happens if there is no longer a Soviet threat?'[5]

Despite occasional ministerial rhetoric about the Western Alliance's long-term commitment to the transformation of East-West relations, the assumptions underlying British security policy have until now included an expectation of continuing confrontation between East and West well into the twenty-first century – contained on the Western side by an Atlantic Alliance within which the United States will remain the dominant partner, contributing both a nuclear guarantee and a substantial conventional contingent to the European continent. Such a set of assumptions provides underlying stability for British foreign policy as a whole. In an Atlantic system within which a divided Europe depends upon American protection and reinforcement, the United Kingdom can be seen as holding a pivotal position. No longer quite the bridge between the United States and Europe which British ministers were so fond of describing twenty or thirty years ago, it is still a vital link in America's capacity to reinforce the central front, and America's major partner in keeping the Atlantic sea lanes open and the Atlantic skies free from Soviet attack.

Movement in East-West relations, however gradual, brings a different set of concerns to the fore. If there is a realistic prospect of moving from confrontation through detente to the eventual establishment of a peaceful order within Europe, what kind of order would the British government prefer? How rapidly – or how cautiously – should it seek to move towards it? What are the mechanisms with which it should negotiate the long and difficult process of mutual adjustment? How cautious ought Britain and its allies to be in maintaining their defences, both nuclear and conventional, during the long transition – and how should it persuade its taxpayers of the need for continuing defence efforts in the face of an apparently declining threat? What elements of its nuclear and conventional forces is Britain prepared to dismantle, and in what order, through the negotiated process of arms control? What are the implications of such a gradual transformation for the established Atlantic relationship – and what are the long-term implications for Britain's position in the world?

The formal answers to some of these questions were provided for the Nato member governments over twenty years ago, as the Alliance came to terms with an earlier period of detente. 'The ultimate purpose of the Alliance', the Harmel Report declared, 'is to achieve a just and lasting peaceful order in Europe accompanied by appropriate security guarantees': not to be a permanent pillar of the international order, that is, but to contain the Soviet Union until the evolution of its society, its economy and its relations with the East European countries have made it possible to construct the stable European order which the Allies failed to achieve in the traumatic conditions of 1945–8.[6] The Harmel Report, once accepted, provided the multilateral framework for West Germany's pursuit of *Ostpolitik*, which moved Europe a small but significant distance along the road from the entrenched hostility of the cold war – of two armed camps divided by the Iron Curtain – towards renewed international cooperation. Harmel had made clear the centrality of Germany, both to Western Europe's present security – as the provider of the largest single contingent of conventional forces and as the central front – and to the achievement of the long-term goal of a stable political order. 'No final and stable settlement in Europe is possible without a solution of the German question which lies at the heart of present tensions in Europe. Any such settlement must end the unnatural barriers between Eastern and Western Europe, which are most clearly and cruelly manifested in the division of Germany.'[7]

For the moment, and for the foreseeable future, a Soviet threat remains, in the concentration of Soviet conventional forces in central Europe and in the weight of Soviet nuclear forces targeted on Western Europe and on Western Europe's ally, the United States. The achievement of the Intermediate Nuclear Forces Treaty, after West European governments demonstrated their determination to deploy modernized intermediate nuclear weapons, has reinforced the underlying theme of Harmel: that the pursuit of detente is only possible on the basis of continuing deterrence, which both maintains the confidence that derives from military balance and exerts sufficient pressure on the USSR to make the concessions the West seeks. Detente policy, and the issues involved in maintaining adequate Western defences, will be discussed further below. We should, however, note three associated and subsidiary threats to British and West European stability: that of instability in Eastern Europe, that of a decline in the American commitment to European security, and that of disorder outside Europe spilling over into a confrontation between the two superpowers, which face each other across Europe.

Political instability and economic weakness in Eastern Europe present intractable problems, not only for the Soviet Union but also, less directly, for Western Europe. A catastrophic collapse of order, leading to a Soviet military intervention, in any East European country would halt or reverse the slow shuffle back towards peaceful relations between the two halves of Europe. Economic reform is essential to the regeneration of Eastern Europe's inefficient and over-centralized economies. Yet shifts towards more realistic pricing mechanisms threaten its fragile political orders; and economic decentralization threatens the central role of the Communist Party.

The Soviet Union and the Western allies therefore have a degree of common interest in encouraging a gradual process of liberalization in Eastern Europe – even though the long-term objectives of Moscow diverge from those of Brussels, Bonn, Paris, London and Washington. The Western response must be carefully orchestrated among the major Western governments and, given the importance of the economic dimension to Eastern Europe, it must be orchestrated through the European Community as much as through Nato and WEU. British interests and priorities need to be reconciled with and coordinated with those not only of the Americans, but also of the French and the Italians (with their particular historical and current interests in Eastern Europe), and, above all, of the West Germans, who have the most at stake in re-establishing human, economic and political links with the rest of central Europe.

Even before the Moscow summit of June 1988 led President Reagan to declare that 'we are beginning to take down the barriers of the postwar era', a number of developments were sapping the American commitment to transatlantic defence. 'Europe no longer dominates American thinking as much as it did in the past,' Sir Geoffrey Howe remarked in March 1987, pointing to 'trends in American thinking which might diminish our security – perhaps not today or tomorrow, but possibly in the longer term'.[8] These trends include the attraction for Americans of reducing their vulnerability to nuclear attack, evident in the appeal of the Strategic Defence Initiative (SDI) and in the American approach to the Reykjavik summit. They also include persistent demands for West European countries to increase their share of the burden of Alliance conventional defence, linked to demands to reduce the 330,000 American forces committed to Europe. The change of presidency in 1988, and the struggle to reduce the budget deficit, are likely further to increase pressures for reduction. Few informed commentators expect the number of US forces in central Europe in the late 1990s to remain within reach of current levels.

Robert Hunter has recently suggested that the US is undergoing 'a major shift' in 'the underlying psychology of relations with Europe', resulting from a redirection of its attention from Europe to East Asia and the Third World, and from increasing irritation with its European allies over political differences, Nato burden-sharing, trading practices and economic competition.[9] The risk for the West Europeans is that such a shift will result in troop withdrawals and a review of the established patterns of Western security much faster than the parallel shift in East-West relations will result in agreed reductions of forces on both sides. Here again careful coordination of policies and of defence priorities among West European governments will be necessary to assure the Americans of Western Europe's substantial contributions to the common defence, and to balance the gradual reduction of American forces against the pace of progress in arms control and confidence-building between the two halves of Europe.

American military concern has turned increasingly to the threats which direct and indirect Soviet actions pose outside Europe. There follows from this a further source of instability within the Western Alliance, which stems from the difference of perception between Western Europe and the United States about the causes of regional conflict and the appropriate Western response: this was already evident during the Vietnam War, but became most severe as a problem in transatlantic relations over the Arab-Israeli conflict and the response to international terrorism.[10] Britain, as a loyal ally claiming a special relationship with the United States, has been subject to intense cross-pressures in particular crises. But British public opinion, and by and large also British governments, have felt themselves closer to the prevailing West European view – on the conflict in Lebanon, on the sources of instability in Central America, on the crisis in Grenada – than to the conventional wisdom of Washington.

Threats to international order are the concern of the whole international community. Britain's withdrawal from East of Suez in the late 1960s sharply reduced its extra-European military reach. The commitment of the UK's marine force to the northern flank and of its navy to the northeast Atlantic focused its attention on regions where the Soviet threat was the only challenge, as compared with the complicated uncertainties of Mediterranean security and Nato's southern flank. The Falklands campaign took British forces back outside the Nato area in strength, under exceptional circumstances. More modestly and more frequently, British naval and land contingents have found themselves committed to operations in the Sinai, the Red Sea, Lebanon and the Gulf, while British military missions continue to operate in southern Africa. Except in southern Africa, where Britain's historical responsibilities and local familiarity make for a special role, these responses to regional disorder have generally been part of a European reaction to American pressure for burden-sharing. The Gulf is an interesting case, as a British naval patrol of several years' standing was associated during 1987 with a European force loosely gathered under the umbrella of WEU. Instability in the Mediterranean may well become a distinctively European concern in the course of the 1990s, with the continuing Arab-Israeli conflict and the demographic explosion in Egypt and North Africa imposing increasing strains on national economies and societies, threatening to spill migration and political disorder onto the northern shores.

None of these threats, it may be repeated, are to Britain alone. As with the economic dimension of British foreign policy, the national framework of strategic policy has become progressively blurred, caught up within the broader pattern of West European and transatlantic security. The security of the United Kingdom is part of the security of Western Europe, to which Britain must make an appropriate contribution. The maintenance of international order against the threats posed by local conflicts, revolution and international terrorist groups is an international public good, to which – again – Britain should contribute, alongside others, its appropriate share.

Defence and foreign policy

A country's defence posture is not simply a matter of calculated responses to carefully weighed threats. Defence is at the heart of British foreign policy: not only because the military instrument remains the ultimate support for foreign policy objectives, but also because of the important contribution which military power and pride make towards a nation's view of itself. The strength of popular support for the maintenance of a British independent nuclear deterrent force has not been diminished by perceptions of a weakening Soviet threat. The rationale for a British deterrent had, after all, as much to do with the preservation of Britain's international standing as a world power as with the intensity of the Soviet threat as then perceived. Together with the East of Suez commitment, it gave Britain the right to claim a special place in the counsels of Washington, and a seat 'at the top table' in international diplomacy. The powerful symbolic association of military power with national pride was demonstrated again by the Falklands War, which fostered the image, both at home and abroad, of Britain as a country with a strong government and a clear sense of direction.

In the absence of any regular report to Parliament from the Foreign and Commonwealth Office, the Defence White Paper serves as the main annual statement on the objectives of British foreign policy. There are four arenas of foreign policy in which Britain's defence effort is used to underpin the political and diplomatic activities which are an intrinsic part of its (and Nato's) dual approach, 'seeking political dialogue and greater understanding alongside deterrence and defence'.[11] They are the United States, where Britain seeks to influence US policy and to maintain the American commitment to transatlantic defence; Western Europe, where it demonstrates its European credentials and maintains its claim to be a major European player; the Soviet Union, where it ensures that Britain remains a power to be bargained with; and, at the margins, the rest of the world, where Britain's international standing may be raised by retaining residual military commitments, missions and training assistance programmes, as well as by selling equipment and 'showing the flag'.

Maintaining a special relationship with the United States was a fundamental objective of postwar British policy. At the outset that relationship was as much political and economic as military, resting upon the shared interests of the world's two reserve currencies and the shared outlook of the two countries' foreign policy elites. In the late 1980s the special quality of the relationship is evident primarily in the military sphere, above all in nuclear weapons and intelligence collaboration. In both these fields Britain gains a great deal from the relationship. In return it provides for a network of US bases which is vital to the maintenance of the US commitment to Europe, and it plays the part of America's most loyal partner within the Alliance. Of America's European allies Britain alone implemented the 3%

69

target for annual increases in defence spending, agreed in response to US pressure in 1979. For the following six years it carried a sustained increase in military spending, which at one point brought its absolute defence expenditure above the level of both France and Germany. Of America's European allies Britain alone agreed to the use of air bases on its soil for the US raid on Libya in 1986.

The Anglo-American special relationship has served British interests well for over forty years. It has provided the UK both with its own nuclear deterrent at reduced cost to its defence budget, and with a useful accretion of international influence and respect, in return for Britain's acceptance of an unavoidable strategic dependence on US military power. However, the assumptions and personal relations on which it rested in the postwar years have faded. The special quality of the relationship was always more important – and more evident – in London than in Washington. And Washington no longer discriminates so naturally between the Anglo-Saxon link and the US-European relationship as a whole. The loyal ally may indeed risk being taken for granted while attention is paid to the more difficult and demanding partners within the Alliance. Germany is now America's most important European security partner – the key to agreed changes in strategy and to agreed moves on arms reductions or weapons modernization. Britain and France follow Germany in importance, as Europe's two nuclear powers and the two other suppliers of substantial conventional forces in Germany.

This is not to argue that the British government should deliberately loosen its ties to the United States. Rather, it is to suggest that it should abandon the illusion that the special relationship is more than a set of limited arrangements, and should approach the UK-US link with a more hard-headed calculation of the costs and benefits to Britain. There is a risk of circularity in the current rationale, in which increased defence expenditure – and particular obligations in the defence field – are justified with reference to the privileged access these acquire in Washington, but where the access gained does not extend significantly beyond the fields of defence and intelligence, in which the extra expenditure is made. The US commitment is to Western Europe as a whole, and American policy-makers look to the West Europeans – and, increasingly, also to the Japanese – to share their regional and global security burdens. The particular size and distribution of Britain's defence effort no longer singles it out in Washington, in terms of overall influence on American policy, from its European partners.

Since the completion of the withdrawal from East of Suez in 1970, Britain's defence effort has been focused overwhelmingly on Western Europe and the east Atlantic. Capitalizing on this shift, Defence Secretary Denis Healey joined with Helmut Schmidt in launching the Eurogroup, to symbolize both in Washington and in the capitals of the European continent the contribution which Britain, together with its European partners, was now making to the common defence. Edward Heath as Prime Minister considered the potential political value of Britain's military forces when negotiating British entry to the European Community, though on that occasion Anglo-French conversations about nuclear collaboration did not progress beyond the tentative stage.

Since then British governments have by and large underplayed the political significance of their country's contribution to European security. They have left it to France to highlight – and to gain political capital from – its contribution (smaller than Britain's) to the defence of Germany, and to invest the creation of a Franco-German brigade with all the significance of a major step forward in European integration. The British government has seldom sought to portray the 55,000 British forces on the central front as a direct British contribution to Germany, as well as to the Alliance as a whole. Still less has it sought to portray British nuclear weapons, both nuclear and tactical, as providing extended deterrence to Germany should the US guarantee fail – which has become an active topic in the debate in France and Germany over the role of the French deterrent. Few in Britain or elsewhere are aware of the degree of cooperation achieved between Britain's armed forces and those of its Continental neighbours, most marked in the naval field and in the operation of the Anglo-Dutch marine force.[12] Britain's substantial, even disproportionate, contribution to European defence has appeared in the past to be intended to impress Washington more than to gain credit in Paris or Bonn.

There are a number of reasons why it may become more difficult within the next four years to maintain the political balance of British defence policy between Washington and Bonn. The Atlantic priority points towards a strong navy; the Continental commitment, towards the maintenance of major land and air forces in Germany. Rising equipment costs and budgetary pressures will make it difficult for

Britain to afford both; one or the other will have to take priority. West European security cooperation is moving ahead, through WEU, the Eurogroup and the Independent European Programme Group, with the British government committing itself alongside its French and German partners 'to develop a more cohesive European defence identity', to quote the *Platform on European Security Interests,* agreed by WEU foreign and defence ministers in October 1987. 'It is our conviction', the *Platform* continues,

> that a more united Europe will make a stronger contribution to the Alliance, to the benefit of Western security as a whole ... We remain determined to pursue European integration including security and defence and [thereby to] make a more effective contribution to the common defence of the West.

Yet the British government, and the British armed services, have nevertheless retained a certain ambivalence about the compatibility of closer West European cooperation with Atlantic solidarity. The Prime Minister in particular has expressed her misgivings about the emergence of 'substructures' within the Alliance, represented above all by the structure of Franco-German defence cooperation. London remains attentive to messages from Washington which express doubt or disapproval about closer European cooperation on matters from SDI to armaments cooperation. The declared concern is to avoid giving any indication to Washington of declining West European loyalty to the Atlantic Alliance, which might set off the reduction in the American commitment which West European governments fear. But there is a danger that Britain will find itself reluctantly following a process of development of closer defence and security cooperation, the terms of which will have been set by other European governments, while finding itself less and less able to carry weight in Washington as the American administration adjusts its security relationship with continental Europe. In the long run, if and as the East-West confrontation fades, an older European pattern of international relations may re-emerge. Britain will then find itself no longer the pivot of the transatlantic security system, but the western border of an integrating Europe of which Germany will once again be the centre.

From the perspective of Moscow, Britain is one of Western Europe's three leading Atlantic Alliance members, and one of its two nuclear powers. If and as negotiations to reduce strategic nuclear weapons between the superpowers move forward, Britain and France will share concerns about the potential impact of further reductions on their national deterrent forces and on the security of Western Europe as a whole. Both governments will share with the Federal Republic an active concern over the delicate balance between security and detente and between nuclear and conventional deterrence, as the climate of East-West relations changes. Geographical and historical links will make it easier for these three to reconcile their priorities, as the current structure of European security begins to crumble, than to reconcile the priorities of any individual European power with the distinctive global and regional interests of the United States.

Over the past fifteen years British governments have moved a long way towards coordinating their approach to the Soviet Union and to Eastern Europe with their West European partners through EPC. Since 1984 they have begun, more slowly and painfully, to coordinate European approaches to defence and security through the seven-nation framework of WEU. Soviet leaders pay attention to British ministers because they see them as representing a leading West European country with a voice that is heard, alongside German and French voices, in Washington. They have paid particular attention in the late 1980s because of the experience and standing of Mrs Thatcher as Prime Minister and because of her close relationship with President Reagan – both personal factors, rather than attributes of Britain's position as such, and not necessarily renewable under different heads of government in Washington and London. The path to continued British influence, in Moscow and in the capitals of Eastern Europe, will therefore lie in a mixture of bilateral and multilateral initiatives, in which the coordination of West European policies will be a precondition of the exertion of influence.

The postwar rationale for the deployment of British forces outside the North Atlantic area rested upon residual imperial commitments and the obligations of Britain's status as a world power. The status which Britain retains as a permanent member of the UN Security Council and, alongside France, as a European power with extra-European responsibilities may be seen to have been bolstered by the occasional projection of military power. But constraints upon resources have reduced the available forces to token size. It is open to question whether the governments of Africa or Latin America are more impressed with the image of national strength presented by a British frigate or a German car, a Japanese computer or a Chinese satellite, in a world in which economic and technological capacity have come to count as much as military capability. The rescue of the crew of the *Hyundai Seven* by a Royal Navy frigate in the Persian Gulf in 1987 was a gesture briefly appreciated in Korea, but without any impact on the export drive of Hyundai into British markets or on the policy of the Korean government. Nor is there any evident link between the protection of reflagged Kuwaiti tankers by British warships and the operations of the Kuwait Investment Office in London. Military power and contributions to the common defence remain useful national assets in transatlantic relations and in the multilateral politics of Western Europe. However, they no longer have much value for the country which wields them outside those spheres.

Commitments, capabilities and costs
Defence is a field in which governments have to take a long-term perspective. Rapid changes of direction are difficult and extremely expensive. Major weapons systems procured through national development and production may take ten years or more from initial decision to entry into service. Some time can be saved by buying 'off the shelf' from abroad, but this can upset a country's balance of payments and damage its industrial base. Once in service, they are likely to remain operational for a further fifteen to twenty-five years. Governments must therefore struggle to anticipate future changes, both among adversaries and among allies. And they must start with the commitments they have trained and equipped for, and the capabilities they have acquired to meet them.

Alone among Nato's European member states, Britain currently contributes to all four elements of Western military capabilities:

(1) nuclear deterrence, through both its strategic submarine-based force and its tactical aircraft-based nuclear capacity;
(2) conventional defence of the European mainland, through BAOR and RAF Germany;
(3) defence of transatlantic resupply routes, through naval and air forces committed to the eastern Atlantic and through marine and air forces committed to the defence of northern Norway; and

(4) out-of-area operations, through forces trained and deployed outside Europe and through provision of the transport capacities needed to support them.

In addition it devotes significant resources to the defence of the United Kingdom, protecting not only its territorial integrity but also the military bases and installations and resupply routes which are vital to the transatlantic security link.

All of these commitments are valued by our allies, both European and North American. By and large, they take it for granted that Britain will continue to supply this spread of forces. But the cost of maintaining them over the next ten years and more is likely to prove unacceptable to the British public, even on the most optimistic assumptions about Britain's future growth rate and the capacity of the UK economy to bear the burden. The bulk of the costs of the Trident force will fall on the budget over the next five years. Following that, and overlapping with it, will come a costly succession of re-equipment programmes: for the navy, a rolling programme of ship replacement, including the replacement of the two assault ships which support the northern flank reinforcement role; for the air force, the completion of the Tornado programme, with the ambitious joint European Fighter Aircraft programme now getting under way; and, for the army, a large number of less costly re-equipment programmes, including the provision of a new battle tank.

The Conservative government which took office in 1979 was determined to apply the hard test of national interest in Britain's acceptance of international responsibilities. This robust attitude has been evident in the British approach to the budgetary and agricultural policies of the European Community, as well as to the less efficient international organizations within the UN framework. It has not yet been applied to the defence sector. Yet a firm British commitment to the maintenance of Western security and international order is not incompatible with a more robust attitude to Britain's share of that defence burden. There is no intrinsic reason why the United Kingdom should contribute more than its fair share to the defence of the Baltic approaches, or of the central front, any more than it should contribute more than its fair share to the agricultural support costs of the European Community, from which Denmark, for example, benefits very considerably, while Germany also balances its budgetary contributions with substantial agricultural benefits. Nor is it self-evident that Britain should continue to shoulder through the coming decades the main responsibility for the initial reinforcement of Norway in a crisis.

The compartmental separation of European Community negotiations from questions of Nato burden-sharing has to some extent disguised the underlying links between them. The contributions to them come out of the same tax revenues, and have not dissimilar impacts upon the domestic economies of net contributors and net beneficiaries. From 1955 until Britain opened negotiations on its revived application to the EC in 1970 the local costs and balance-of-payments effects of the British forces in Germany was a recurrent and contentious issue in German-British relations, with persistent demands from Britain for offset payments and increased contributions to local costs. The long battle to rectify the balance of Britain's costs and benefits within the EC has largely displaced that issue from the intergovernmental agenda. But it should be noted that the 1987 Defence White Paper estimated the invisible transactions related to defence commitments as amounting to a net £1,397 million deficit, of which over £1,000 million was accounted for by local defence expenditure in Germany.

Britain shares the common interest in collective defence. But it also serves its own interests by not doing more than it has to, by not weighing down its economy more than its competitors weigh down theirs. The rapid growth of British defence expenditure, which increased in real terms by £3,000 million between 1978-9 and 1985-6, 'has been a material factor in adding to the tax burden and so to the disincentive effects of taxation'.[13] The defence industry is also skill-intensive, absorbing a far higher proportion of British research and development in advanced technology than it does in the case of any of Britain's main competitors. After the cumulative increases of 1979-86, defence expenditure is planned to fall by some 6% in real terms in 1987-9, relieving the burden on tax revenues a little, but widening the gap between requirements and supply. 'The ending of the commitment to maintain real growth inevitably means that difficult choices have to be made between priorities in our forward plans,' the 1988 Defence White Paper soberly admits.

Britain therefore finds itself with an overstretched defence budget in a strategic environment which is likely to change significantly during the next five to ten years. Major changes in Britain's defence commitments or deployment would themselves threaten to destabilize further an already unsettled military and political balance. Indeed it has been, and remains, a strong argument against any reduction in Britain's conventional forces that British cut-backs might trigger further cuts by the 'less responsible' smaller European allies, and could thus encourage Congressional demands for the withdrawal of US troops from a European partner which would not pay for its own defence. The dilemma is made more acute by the decline in the German birth rate over the past fifteen years, which will make it in any event harder to provide the conventional troop numbers Nato anticipates will be needed in the 1990s.

If arguments against reductions in Britain's conventional commitments are strong, arguments against cutting Britain's nuclear contribution are as strong, if not stronger. Britain's nuclear role remains a vital element in the country's claim to international standing. It commands firm support among the British public. In a period when the prospect of superpower arms reductions poses major uncertainties for European security, and when the credibility of the American nuclear guarantee to Western Europe is increasingly open to question, the justification for a European contribution to the Western Alliance's nuclear deterrent is extremely powerful. Neither the German nor the French governments would wish that European contribution to come solely from France; nor indeed would any other European government.

The British government was on the point of implementing a major defence review in the spring of 1982 when it was overtaken by the Argentine invasion of the Falklands. That review was intended to relieve the strains on defence costs and commitments by reducing the size of the surface navy. This recognized the fundamental political imperatives of the conventional commitment to the European continent and of the nuclear deterrent forces, took into account US naval expansion and anticipated a gradual US troop reduction. In the absence of such a major review, the government has vigorously pursued economies through reforms in the procurement process, producing savings that are useful but small in relation to the widening gap between budgetary allocations and military requirements. The strain is now evident in a gradual postponement of equipment orders and a shrinkage in the number of surface ships available.

It is the harsh judgment of Sir John Nott, the architect of the 1982 review, that 'No British prime minister since the 1960s has been sufficiently devoted to international strategy to think of defence policy within a broader vision of the international system and Britain's place in it.'[14] It is peculiarly difficult to achieve the integration of defence policy within a grand foreign policy design at a time when the strategic and political environment is changing – though John Nott goes on to praise the 'broad conceptualism' of de Gaulle, who redefined French foreign and defence priorities in just such an uncertain and changing environment. It is important to ensure that Britain gains the political credit it deserves from its allies for its substantial contribution, as well as to pursue a progressive redistribution of the relative shares of the defence burden. To be useful in terms of other British interests, that political credit needs to be transferable – at least in principle, in terms of the symbolism and images which are important aspects of foreign policy – to other areas of British external interests, such as international economic management or industrial and technological collaboration.

All of this argues for placing British defence policy within a more explicitly European framework. Britain's commitment to the defence of continental Europe, as the Prime Minister has argued, represents the most tangible and substantial evidence of its willingness to shoulder and share in the common responsibilities of Western Europe within the Western Alliance. Denis Healey and Edward Heath, in the years between the decision to withdraw from East of Suez and British accession to the European Community, both used the commitment of virtually all Britain's armed forces to Western Europe to symbolize the shift their governments were making in international economic and foreign policy. Their successors, their eyes more firmly fixed on Washington, have hesitated to make either symbolic or practical links between defence commitments and the other dimensions of foreign policy.

There is as yet no effective 'European pillar' of the sort envisaged by President Kennedy in his call for a greater European share in the Alliance a quarter of a century ago. We are faced with an untidy tangle of overlapping organizations, in the creation of most of which Britain has played an active part, supplemented by a further tangle of bilateral and *ad hoc* multilateral arrangements. The diversity of national inhibitions – French, Danish, Greek, even German and British – about the full acceptance of collective European defence responsibilities makes it impossible to bring all European Nato members within a single, all-encompassing framework. The non-congruity of EC and Nato membership similarly inhibits the pulling together of civil and military technological cooperation, and leaves a degree of awkwardness in the coordination of policy on East-West relations and the Middle East within EPC. The most convenient vehicle available is WEU, which brings together the major European powers and includes all those European countries which contribute directly to the central front. Bilateral incrementalism – strengthening existing cooperation through practical initiatives with West Germany, the Netherlands, France, Italy and Belgium – is a necessary supplement to this. The more active a role that Britain plays within this process of creating a European pillar, the greater its ability to ensure that it develops as a counterbalance to the United States within the Alliance – as Kennedy intended – and not as an alternative.

The British government has moved some considerable way in this direction since the early 1980s. The British response to the revitalization of the defence dimension of the Franco-German Treaty in 1982 led first to a tripartite meeting of defence ministers and then to the relaunching of WEU. Michael Heseltine as Defence Minister championed the Independent European Programme Group as a vehicle for coordinating European approaches to military procurement. During the course of 1987–8 an active Franco-British dialogue on defence was getting under way, with a number of new bilateral agreements. British ministers and officials were also pushing hard to improve and upgrade the structure of WEU. Much less progress had yet been made in explaining to Parliament or to the public the rationale for doing so.

The pressures of rising costs and limited budgets affect Britain's Continental partners as well as itself. Greater integration of national defence efforts offers *some* prospect of containing costs, by sharing procurement and logistical and training facilities, and by obtaining a degree of specialization among national roles. The savings achieved through intergovernmental collaboration are, however, limited by the requirements of *juste retour* and the time-consuming procedures of national negotiation and national accountability. The unfavourable comparison of West European and American defence costs and deployments, which shows that West European governments as a whole spend more to deploy fewer forces which are less well-equipped, could only be overcome by a much greater degree of integration than is yet in prospect – and at the political cost of abandoning national sovereignty in its most sensitive and symbolic sphere. There are nevertheless some useful economies to be made through bilateral and multilateral sharing; and the learning curve of joint procurement is also slowly reducing the cost of shared equipment. Even in the nuclear field bilateral Franco-British cooperation can provide some improved ability to carry out tasks at containable cost. Franco-British defence cooperation, both conventional and nuclear, also serves other and wider purposes. As a complement to Franco-German cooperation it helps to reintegrate France into Western defence, bringing the three leading West European powers together in managing the complexities of European security. Further progress in negotiations between the superpowers to reduce levels of nuclear deterrent forces will necessitate close consultation between Britain and France on their appropriate response as nuclear weapons states, and consultation also between both governments and the Federal Republic on the future role of nuclear weapons in European security.

Advanced technology cannot be neatly separated into military and civil compartments. The computer which can assist in organizing management information or air traffic can also play a part in controlling the battlefield – as the United States has forcefully reminded its allies in tightening controls on the transfer of technology. The same space launcher serves to lift telecommunications satellites and military satellites. The research and development needed to produce airframes and aero-engines overlaps the military and the civil domain. Britain, in contrast, for example, to France, retains a separate policy-making structure for national and collaborative research and development, institutionalized in the MoD and the DTI. Here, as in other areas of international relations, British governments have not taken a strategic approach, preferring in most cases to take each decision on its own merits as these appear at the time. In 1986–7 the MoD was pursuing closer European procurement collaboration at the same time as the DTI was resisting new proposals for collaboration on grounds of cost. Nor did DTI policy towards mergers and takeovers appear to take account of the developing European procurement dimension. In both civil and military high technology, national solutions are increasingly unrealistic. The cheapest alternative in most immediate instances is to buy from the United States – or on occasion, in civil technology, from Japan. But the accumulation of such purchases is resisted, not unnaturally, because of the erosion of British industrial, and research-and-development, capacity which they imply. Such a gradual erosion is most strongly resisted in the military sphere, since it implies a loss of the capacity to maintain national defence, and thus to maintain national sovereignty. The uncomfortable choice offered is increasingly between dependence on the United States and integration within a West European framework. It would be easier for British policy-makers to assess that choice, decision by decision, if the contexts for the government's research-and-development, competition and industrial support policies were harmonized.

The best long-term prospect for reducing the burden of British defence expenditure without jeopardizing Britain's security lies in progress towards easier relations between Eastern and Western Europe, and thus towards lower levels of armed forces on both sides of the European divide. That involves collaboration above all, first within the West European frameworks of WEU and EPC, then within the Western Alliance, then within the hard bargaining (and discreet manoeuvring) of East-West negotiations. The weapons which threaten our security are on East European or Soviet soil. The concessions we have to trade in return are most often forces in place on the European continent, of which British forces form only a part. The focus for British security policy over the next decade and more will be primarily on central Europe, where the cold war began, and on Germany and its future role in European security, politics and economic cooperation.

6

THE INTANGIBLE ELEMENTS OF FOREIGN POLICY

The most distinctively national elements in the interdependent world of the 1990s will in many ways be those provided by national values and cultures, and the efforts made by governments to promote and protect them. Britain's international standing and influence will depend not only upon its economic success and military strength, but also upon its reputation: that is, the image which foreign governments and their publics have of Britain, of the qualities of its government and diplomacy, the stability of its society, the richness of its culture and the strength of its political and social values.

The degree of influence which any British government now has over the transmission of such images in a world of mass communications is limited. It is difficult to avoid controversy over which strengths any government should play to, or which impressions it should strive to counteract. What is nevertheless clear is that British governments have been uncertain about the appropriate level of activity in this field, and the distinctive values they should attempt to stress, ever since their first plunge into propaganda in World War I – in contrast to their French counterparts, who have consistently emphasized France's cultural and human values in the rhetoric, and sometimes too in the substance, of foreign policy.

The recovery of self-confidence from the low point of the late 1970s has been reflected in a more optimistic interpretation, by both ministers and officials, of the advantages to be gained from building on Britain's intangible assets in foreign policy. (Comparison with the pessimistic assessment of the CPRS quoted in Chapter 2 is interesting.) The Prime Minister has repeatedly underlined the importance of British values, and of respect in other countries for those values, in strengthening Britain's international position. 'Britain enjoys far greater influence in the world than any cold assessment of its economic and defence strength might suggest,' the FCO boldly minuted the House of Commons Foreign Affairs Committee in November 1986. And it continued:

> The Government believes it is a proper use of public funds to sponsor programmes and activities designed to win respect and understanding for Britain and the British way of life, as well as to disseminate information about British policies and interests at home and abroad. If the United Kingdom wishes to be treated as an important and responsible member of the international community; if she wishes to be seen as a technologically advanced, modern and successful country; if she wishes citizens of other nations to share in a rich cultural heritage stretching back over many centuries; and if she wishes to be seen as a nation which practises the values she preaches – of freedom, democracy, and integrity in public life: she must ensure that her image abroad serves those ends.[1]

The international image of an open society depends primarily on how foreign governments and their publics see that society through the medium of their own public and private communications networks. The British government can alter such perceptions only at the margin, by acting to inform and educate opinion-leaders in other countries about British values, objectives and policies. It cannot, for example, prevent the troubles in Northern Ireland creating an adverse impression abroad. But it can legitimately work to present the British government's response to those troubles in the best possible light, and to correct and counter misleading reports in foreign media. 'Cultural relations' are rather like prestige advertising, justified less by the specific outcome of each presentation than by the accumulation of goodwill, and the gradual construction of a positive image for a country's government, economy and domestic society. Britain's self-image, low in the late 1970s, has improved significantly over the decade. But the shift of attitudes has been slower in other countries; impressions of social conflict, industrial decline and a country living in its past linger on.

Most important, a country's domestic society constitutes the essential non-economic resources for its foreign policy, providing attitudes which reinforce or undermine a government's international efforts, as well as expertise on which governments can draw, and links with other societies. Those links have grown exponentially since the war, as international travel has mushroomed, migration has become a global phenomenon (and problem), and radio and television have come to provide a sense of immediacy and involvement in distant countries. Britain has become cosmopolitan, not only in the operations of its financial markets and the international integration of its industry, but also in the diversity of cultural influences and languages within its population. That in turn raises difficult questions about its national identity and international role – two features which provide the key to a country's foreign policy.

The promotion of British values

No British government in peacetime has ever precisely defined the values which it wishes to promote through the cultural, educational and information instruments available to it in the international arena. The FCO Memorandum of November 1986 talks of seeking 'to convey the image of Britain as a creative, well-integrated and forward-looking society based on liberal values – a social and cultural model to be emulated and trusted'. It talks also of projecting 'a society in which high technology plays an important role', of promoting 'knowledge of the British system of government and of the principles underpinning it' and thus of 'promoting British democratic values'. Mrs Thatcher has laid particular stress, since she became Prime Minister, on promoting the principle of economic liberty as a necessary condition for political liberty, which Britain must demonstrate to other countries 'by word and by deed'. 'In the long run,' she has argued, 'the ideas we offer are more important than the aid we give' to 'the true interests of the poorer nations'.[2] Education, information, the example of a thriving economy and a stable society are thus important elements in Britain's contribution to the international order.

The instruments available to the government with which to make this contribution include the British Council, the External Services of the BBC, the Central Office of Information (COI) and a range of government-funded schemes for encouraging students from abroad to study in Britain. Britain spends substantially less on all of these than the German government, and much less than the French and Japanese governments on all except external broadcasting. The British Council has undergone seventeen outside reviews of its functions and funding between 1947 and 1986 – clear evidence of political uncertainty about its appropriate role. After a number of reductions in its budget in the public expenditure reviews of the mid-1970s, it saw a further reduction in real terms of nearly 20% between 1978–9 and 1987–8.[3] BBC External Services have been reviewed nine times over the same period. After years of financial retrenchment and deteriorating audibility, it was agreed in 1980 to allocate an additional £100 million in capital funds over the ten-year period 1981–91 to upgrading its transmitters, allowing it to compete more effectively with the heavy investment in modern equipment of the Americans and West Germans, among friendly powers, and of the Russians, East Germans and North Koreans, among hostile powers.

The ending of subsidized fees in higher education for overseas students, in 1980, saved the Treasury £100 million, and led both to a fall in numbers and to a redirection of the flow, as universities and colleges went out to recruit those who could be persuaded to pay the full cost. The 'Pym Package', announced in February 1983, allocated £46 million to the FCO for targeted scholarship schemes, aimed at potential leaders and decision-makers in specific countries; a further £100,000 was allocated to the British Council for the promotion of British higher education overseas. The COI has been a candidate for privatization on a number of occasions.

Paradoxically, therefore, a greater emphasis on the role of ideas and values in British foreign policy has been accompanied by a reduction in the availability of the instruments to pursue them. This is partly due to uncertainty over how far government action is necessary in this area. Values are arguably best promoted by private initiative and example; ideas and education may thrive best in the market-place. There is a general Western interest in counteracting the vigorous activities of the Soviet Union and its allies, but the specific British interests which justify giving a higher priority to public expenditure in this field are less self-evident. The predominance of English as the international language of communication provides a demand for English education, culture, publications and language teaching which will not – it is argued – be deterred by full-cost charging. The contrast with the Reagan administration is, however, striking. Commitment in Washington to private initiative and open markets was accompanied by substantial increases in government funding for the promotion of American values abroad and for those US agencies which support cultural exchanges, assist non-Americans to study in the USA, and provide the American point of view in international media and to foreign publics. In addition the Reagan administration sponsored the establishment of the federally funded National Endowment for Democracy to encourage the spread of democratic ideas in other countries. Modelled on the West German party foundations, its four associated bodies include Republican and Democratic institutes for international affairs.

The contribution of the BBC to Britain's international image and reputation is unchallengeable. A 1985 survey by a Paris-based international consortium of Soviet listeners' reactions to foreign broadcasts showed the BBC far ahead of American, German, Canadian and Swedish networks in its reputation for accuracy, immediacy and balance.[4] It received over 500,000 letters from listeners in other countries in 1987, and nearly as many in 1986. There is strong evidence that elite audiences – and government leaders – in a great many countries turn first to the BBC as a source of information when crises blow up.

It also claims to be 'the largest language-teaching operation in the world', both through direct broadcasting and through programmes made in cooperation with other national networks. It earns substantial royalties from the sales of associated material, selling seventy million copies of an 'English by Radio' booklet in the Hispanic world, five million in China, and one million in West Germany.[5] Its independence from direct British government instructions makes it less a vehicle for British foreign policy than a demonstration of Britain's democratic values. Its reputation depends upon its ability to report criticisms of its own government as well as of foreign governments and their leaders, however painful that may on occasion be to British policy-makers.

The integration of global communications – in particular the gradual displacement of the international radio audience by television, and the prospect of direct television broadcasting by satellite across the world during the 1990s – does, however, pose problems for the British government. BBC External Services were developed first by Sir John Reith in the face of a reluctant Treasury, then by an embattled Britain in the face of German and Italian propaganda broadcasts. They have been maintained since then as a national asset that had already been acquired, which justified the modest costs of preservation and maintenance without necessitating any major new departures. The challenge of the 1990s will be more subtle, but will require difficult decisions on the appropriate extent of government involvement and funding in a changing communications market. The total cost of BBC External Services in 1986–7, including the monitoring services which listen in to and analyse foreign broadcasts (thus serving the FCO and the security services as well as the BBC itself), was £112 million. 'We therefore spend on the defence of ideas 0.6% of what we devote to physical defence', the BBC pointedly told the Foreign Affairs Committee.

We are already witnessing the development of global communications conglomerates, which are aiming to take advantage of the new technology to transmit news and entertainment across national boundaries. The size and profitability of the American market will give a built-in advantage to groups which are strong there, and will lend an 'Americocentric' orientation to much of their output.[6] Governments elsewhere will continue to regulate their national markets to protect what they see as their cultural autonomy from the invasion of Anglo-Saxon cosmopolitanism. The British government will have to decide how far it wishes to promote a distinctively British perspective in this international market, and what mix of policies and expenditure is the best means of so doing.

The US administration has acted to take advantage of the new technical possibilities by developing its 'Worldnet' TV channel, already available from satellite throughout North and South America, and due to be extended to the Middle East, Africa and Asia by 1990. The BBC in its turn put forward proposals for a half-hour television 'World News' bulletin in 1987, combining the technical resources of BBC Television with the editorial network of BBC External Services, to be available for rebroadcasting by local television stations. It established that a considerable worldwide demand for the programme existed, created by the BBC's existing reputation and by the appetite of new broadcast and cable channels for material. It requested an additional £1 million a year to launch this new service. The government's refusal, on the grounds that 'a British commercial world television news service has been started without public funds and ... that the provision of puhlic funds to the BBC for this purpose would not be justified', echoed a previous government's dusty answer to Lord Reith's original proposal for the BBC World Service fifty-six years before. Hostility to the BBC from within the Conservative Party and the government, strengthened by a number of differences over the previous five years, did not help the External Services' case. The ministerial announcement that the request had been refused was greeted with cheers from some Conservative MPs.[7]

The British Council has both a more modest reputation and a more varied range of functions. Struggling under successive changes of emphasis to promote British arts and culture, to promote British exports through knowledge of British design and technology, and to promote technical training and paid educational services for Third World countries, it returned in the late 1970s to an emphasis on English-language teaching, earning a substantial return in several southern European countries by so doing. How far this is a proper activity for a British government agency is, again, partly a matter of whether it is seen as important to British interests to promote a distinctive national perspective. 'Clearly, one of our great advantages in overseas work is the English language,' a British-based accountancy firm told the Commons Committee. 'The now almost universal acceptance of it as a *lingua franca* is obviously principally due to American influence . . . I believe that one of the key objectives of English cultural diplomacy must be to seek to differentiate ourselves from American culture' in the pursuit of both 'international goodwill and long-term economic benefits.'[8]

The demand for English-language teaching, and for education as a whole, has shot up during the past fifteen years. Successive British governments responded to the surge in foreign students during the 1970s by raising the fees charged, largely in response to domestic public spending reviews. The inflow of the late 1970s was highly concentrated, with the United States, Iran, Malaysia, Hong Kong, Nigeria and Iran providing the largest contingents. Many of those who came were from well-to-do families, who could afford the additional costs of full fees. The transformation of the foreign student market in Britain in the early 1980s into a major contributor to the finances of most higher education institutions has indeed demonstrated Britain's continuing competitiveness.

But Britain is not operating in a free market. The United States, for example, provides a wide range of federal and private programmes, which sponsor many of the brightest among the 343,000 foreign students in American universities and colleges. The Japanese government, which played host to some 10,000 students from abroad – overwhelmingly from East and Southeast Asia – in 1987, has announced plans to increase their numbers to 100,000 by the end of the century as an essential element in Japanese foreign policy. The number of students from overseas in British higher education fell by 14% in the three years after the 1980 move to full-cost charging, while numbers in France and Germany rose by nearly 20%. After the 'Pym Package', numbers in Britain again began to rise, reaching a total of 63,500 in 1986, of whom 17,000 were sponsored in some way by government agencies.

The comparative autonomy of British cultural diplomacy, and the intermittent nature of ministerial attention, have inhibited clear definition of political priorities. There has, for example, been no attempt to identify key countries in the way that the German foreign office has done, with its special programmes for France, Israel and, most recently, the United States – this last included because of the importance for German interests of maintaining personal links and understanding with its principal ally through a period when the generation which had come to know Europe during and after World War II was passing into retirement. A four-year special programme, the 'Rippon Package', was introduced in the run-up to British entry to the EC to increase exchanges with the other Community member states; but it was discontinued by the Labour government in 1977. The pattern of British Council spending in the late 1980s still shows the outlines of postwar 're-education', with a continuing higher commitment to Germany than to France. Expenditure in Spain (and in Greece) was higher than in either France or Germany, boosted by the local receipts of successful English-language programmes.

In dealing with shared experiences and values, it is naturally difficult to demonstrate direct benefits from specific expenditures. But the considerable and sustained efforts, first by France, then also by Germany, since the 1950s to promote exchanges of all kinds between the two countries has undoubtedly contributed to the emergence of the Franco-German relationship as a key element in European politics; while the absence of any comparable programme between Britain and either of them has contributed to the sense of a continuing separation between Britain and its major Continental partners. In 1986 the numbers of French and German students in

British higher education were a little over a thousand from each country, compared with some six thousand each way between Germany and France. Within the framework of the European Community the British government was resisting proposals to expand the modest ERASMUS and COMETT schemes, intended to promote wider cooperation between national universities, increased interchange of scholars and students, and specific cooperation in training in high technology.

Britain has much to gain from a targeted cultural policy. If it is the case that the distinctive character and quality of British values is indeed one of the assets which underpins Britain's international influence, then government action should be directed towards impressing those values on the countries most important to British interests. In spite of its more open espousal of British interests as the proper focus for national foreign policy, the Conservative government has since 1979 hesitated to clarify these in the cultural field. It is strong evidence of such lack of clarity that the British Council was spending more in Indonesia in 1986 than in Japan, and more in Ecuador than in Hungary, Czechoslovakia or East Germany.

Britain has not followed its West German or American allies in directly promoting its democratic values through public expenditure abroad. The German government's international activity in this sphere is conducted to a considerable degree through the medium of its political parties and their foundations, which fund conferences and training courses, bringing political leaders to Germany, and even financially assist like-minded parties in other countries. Britain has resisted such overtly political activities, or – beyond the postwar re-education programme – direct political education and propaganda on its own behalf. It has, however, other assets at its disposal, such as symbols of the strength and continuity of its institutions and of its civil traditions – the monarchy most of all, the distinctive English legal system, the armed services. These last have been deployed most actively in the Commonwealth, where they are most familiar, and also in the Middle East. They could be used more fully in other major areas where British interests will be at stake in the next decade, including Western Europe and East Asia. The failure to use the commitment of British forces to central Europe as a symbol of Britain's European presence has already been noted. These forces are also symbols of Britain's commitment, shared with other West European countries, to defend democratic values. Their deploy-

ment, visibility, training in other European languages and cooperation with other Nato forces – all these should be used to demonstrate
that commitment in the broadest sense.

The promotion of democratic values through foreign policy is
most directly demonstrated by government attitudes to human
rights outside Britain. In the nineteenth century the Royal Navy
extended the anti-slavery campaign from Britain to the Atlantic and
Indian Oceans, enforcing basic standards of civilized behaviour.
Gladstone's campaigns for the rights of Bulgarians and others
followed from the same perception that a commitment to individual
liberty could not stop at the water's edge – though the extent of
Britain's responsibility to assist oppressed minorities elsewhere
remained a matter of active political controversy. Human rights
issues are no less controversial or difficult today, though British
governments have far less capability to intervene in the affairs of
other countries. Historical responsibilities – towards Cyprus, Israel,
Hong Kong and, above all, South Africa – leave the British
government open to criticism from abroad on developments over
which Britain's influence is severely limited.

The conflict in southern Africa is likely to remain a major
symbolic issue in international politics for the next decade. The links
with British domestic politics and society are strong, with over a
million citizens of South Africa entitled to claim British citizenship.
Of these, 16,000 moved to Britain in 1986 (more than the total net
inflow of migrants from the Caribbean and Pakistan), and the flow
may well increase if economic, political and security conditions
within South Africa worsen.[9] Britain remains heavily involved in
providing aid and military training to Zimbabwe and has readily
extended its commitments to Mozambique. It has worked closely
with other Western countries, but has also built on the accumulated
experience it has gained in the region and the reputation which the
practical efforts of its representations have won it. As with its
military commitment to central Europe, British policy has been
constructive and responsible, but its presentation has failed to bring
Britain due international credit. Too robust a rejection of the
moralizing hypocrisies of Commonwealth governments has disguised Britain's continuing commitment to protect the Front-Line
States from the damage the conflict inflicts upon them, and to
support – by the limited instruments at its disposal – the principle of
peaceful change within South Africa.

91

British governments, of whatever political persuasion, will wish to continue to demonstrate their active concern about human rights in Eastern Europe and the Soviet Union, ignoring accusations of unwarranted interference in the internal affairs of sovereign states. Consistency, as well as commitment to democratic values, will require them to demonstrate a comparable concern in southern Africa and in Latin America, in circumstances in which Britain's interests and declared principles do not so neatly fit together. Rhetorical gestures, backed up with modest economic assistance, may be the most that can be achieved. But rhetoric and gestures are not without value in the uncertain currency of international politics.

Disillusionment with the Commonwealth has been accentuated by the over-preoccupation of other Commonwealth governments with the South Africa issue, and by their determination to force responsibilities onto Britain that they are reluctant to shoulder themselves. Nevertheless, the Commonwealth connection continues to provide potential assets for Britain to use – in terms of shared language, and educational and legal traditions – which British governments should not allow to wither away. The example of Nigeria, where the determined drive of American international educational policy has substantially displaced British links, while France's targeted cultural and commercial efforts have also made a major impact, shows how Britain's more limited efforts are vulnerable to the competition provided by friendly powers. The shift in Nigeria's external trade towards the US and continental Europe indicates that there are commercial as well as political interests at stake.

The more active a foreign policy Britain wishes to pursue, as a permanent member of the UN Security Council and a European power with a claim to global interests and responsibilities, the more important its presence and visibility in developing countries, using the instruments available to it through diplomatic representation, cultural and educational programmes, and technical and economic assistance. Even if a British government were solely interested in immediate gains and the pursuit of economic interests, it would still be advised to maintain a modest, but active, presence in Third World countries. Thus it would be in a position to bargain with governments over major contracts in competition with companies supported by its major competitor governments, and to provide the cultural and educational underpinning needed – in the face of similar government-sponsored competition – to alert national elites to British technology, design and saleable expertise.

Britain's contributions to the general interests of international development might be left to a greater extent – as some have argued – to private contributions, provided through non-official organizations to combat famine and disease and to support basic education and health care in the poorest countries. There is no real reason why Britain, as one of the world's second-ranking economic powers, should pay more than its appropriate share for this dimension of international public goods; there are no specifically British interests at stake. Indeed, Britain's overseas development aid has shrunk from 0.52% of GNP in 1979 to 0.28% in 1987, leaving the UK well below the OECD average in aid provision. Whereas Japan gave $5,761 million in overseas development aid in 1986, the UK gave only $1,667 million.[10]

But Britain's shared interest in stability and order in the developing world is strong, and is likely to become stronger. Default on international debt by developing countries would damage British banks as well as their overseas competitors, and might destabilize the international economy. Internal disorder and regional conflict overflow into Western Europe in surges of refugees – East African Asians, Vietnam Chinese, Tamils, Iranians. The AIDS virus symbolizes the need for common research and preventive measures against diseases which spread quickly across the world. Weak national governments in countries with weak economies are tempted by the enormous returns offered by the international drugs trade, or find themselves unable to control their own country as the profits of the drugs trade flood in. British interests do not differ from those of its partners in the developed Western world in responding to this range of issues. Nor does the UK have any special or distinctive contribution to offer comparable with the openness to refugees or the use of the navy to combat piracy and slave-trading which characterized nineteenth-century Britain. In these, as in other, areas British foreign policy in the 1990s will be less a distinctively national policy than a contribution to the collective efforts of the advanced industrial world, concerted through the institutions of West European cooperation and the wider institutional frameworks which link Western Europe to the US and Japan.

The domestic context

If British foreign policy is less distinctly British, it is also the case that Britain itself is becoming a less distinct and coherent nation-state. Nineteenth-century industrialization, mass education, newspapers and railways created a nation out of the peoples of the British Isles – a nation with a clear sense of identity and of separation from other nations on the Continent and beyond. Modern mass communications, travel, international industrial and social integration, all have diminished the sense of separateness and thrown into question some aspects of national identity.

In 1968 British residents made 5.5 million journeys abroad, already a sharp increase from the small numbers of the pre- and postwar years. In 1986 they are estimated to have made over 25 million overseas visits: thus up to a third of the British population travelled abroad in the course of a calendar year, with a significant minority making regular and repeated journeys abroad for business

Table 3   Visitors from and to Britain, 1986

Visits abroad by UK residents		Visits to UK, by country of residence	
Top ten countries:			
1 Spain	5,887,000	1 USA	2,288,000
2 France	5,188,000	2 France	1,756,000
3 Ireland	1,657,000	3 West Germany	1,599,000
4 Greece	1,520,000	4 Ireland	984,000
5 West Germany	1,258,000	5 Netherlands	769,000
6 Italy	1,103,000	6 Canada	555,000
7 Portugal	956,000	7 Belgium/Lux.	496,000
8 USA	946,000	8 Italy	494,000
9 Netherlands	868,000	9 Australia	497,000
10 Belgium/Lux.	761,000	10 Sweden	407,000
Regional balance:			
European Community	19,352,000	European Community	6,888,000
Other Western Europe	2,757,000	Other Western Europe	1,413,000
North America	1,167,000	North America	2,843,000
Rest of world	1,905,000	Rest of world	2,699,000

Source: Government Statistical Service, *Business Monitor*, MQ6, Quarter 1, 1987.

and for pleasure. Nearly 90% of these journeys were to Western Europe, from Scandinavia to the Mediterranean (see Table 3). The visitors carried Britain's image and reputation with them, as tourists, businessmen, students and football fans. Nearly 14 million foreign citizens visited Britain in return – 60% of them from Western Europe, 20% from North America – gathering their images of Britain from the streets they walked, the public services they used, and the newspapers they read.

Nearly 2.5 million British residents are now non-white – some 4.5% of the population (see Table 4). Four out of every ten of these are British citizens by birth as well as by upbringing and residence, but most retain sympathies and family ties with other countries, from Grenada and Trinidad to Nigeria, Ghana, India and Pakistan. They include substantial Arab and Chinese communities, less visible than their West Indian or South Asian counterparts but of at least equal importance for Britain's economy and international ties. As Edward Mortimer has noted:

> A striking feature of the London scene in the last ten to twelve years has been the proliferation of Arab newspapers and magazines – in part a consequence of the war in Lebanon, in part reflecting the new oil wealth and the willingness of certain Arab governments and individuals to spend some of it on efforts to influence a broad Arab public opinion. London has to a large extent replaced Beirut as the main meeting point and market place of ideas in the Arab world.[11]

Britain's Muslim population is now larger than its Jewish community, and more numerous in active religious observance than several of the country's major Christian denominations. It includes some of the country's richest inhabitants, as well as many of its poorest.

Alongside these is a growing community of British residents from other European countries, the majority coming to Britain to work and live for a limited period. Their numbers increased by a total of 22,000 in the twelve months from July 1985 to July 1986, which is slightly higher than the net increase from the four countries of South Asia.[12] Several 100,000 Britons were working abroad in return: nearly 50,000 in the Netherlands, a larger number in Germany, with sizeable communities also in Spain, Portugal and the larger Arab states. The presence of some 70,000 British soldiers and airforce

95

Table 4   Ethnic minority populations in Britain, 1984–6 average

Ethnic group	Number (thousands)	UK-born (%)
West Indian or Guyanese	534	53
Indian	760	36
Pakistani	397	42
Bangladeshi	103	31
African	103	35
Chinese	115	24
Arab	66	11
Mixed origin	235	74
Other	119	28
Total non-white group	2,432	43

Source: Government Statistical Service, *Population Trends*, Winter 1987, p. 5.

personnel in Federal Germany for two generations now has led to links which may have long-term social implications, even if as yet they have made only limited political impact. There are British servicemen who were born in Germany and have spent much of their lives there. There is continuing intermarriage and a community of 'stayovers' and civilians sufficiently large for the MoD to have contemplated the possibility of raising Territorial Army units from British citizens in Germany to reinforce regular British forces there.

The erosion of the old boundaries between Britain and abroad has long-term implications for British sovereignty and national autonomy. The erosion is also of the old boundaries between domestic politics and foreign policy. Completion of the Channel Tunnel and progress towards the establishment of a single European market will integrate Britain further with its neighbours. British pensioners are now beginning to travel south to Portugal, Spain and Italy for winter warmth in the same way that their New York counterparts travel to Florida. British lorry-drivers range widely across the European continent and beyond, while Continental juggernauts pound British roads. Domestic policing is becoming caught up in a network of international collaboration, as extradition procedures bring British criminals home from Spain – and British football hooligans return to Belgium to stand trial.

Completion of the internal market will, in effect, mean that Britain yields in most respects control of its own borders in order to gain the benefits of an integrated European economy. The pressures of rising numbers will make effective policing of Britain's borders increasingly difficult, as 25 million journeys a year rise to 50 million and more. That will in time require a European migration policy, replacing national approaches to immigration. The process of European integration will also reduce the distinction between British and other European citizens, as they come to share rights to study, to work and practise their professions, to carry common passport documents and to share many welfare entitlements. The implications of these developments for Britain as an autonomous entity within a broader political and economic system have not yet been addressed.

Government initiatives at home and abroad now interact far more frequently than in the past. The domestic and international image of a government emerges partly out of European summits, partly out of the impact made by its leaders in Washington, Tokyo or Moscow, where they deal with issues at once of direct international and domestic concern, presenting them as best they can to British and foreign audiences through common television pictures. But the impression Britain conveys to other countries now depends as much on the foreign reporting of domestic developments within Britain – urban riots on the one hand, royal weddings on the other – as on the cultural events or official information that the British government may provide in those countries. The damage done to Britain's image on the European continent by the behaviour of a minority of its citizens abroad, whether on holiday or supporting their football teams, has rightly become a matter of government concern at the highest level. When the government attempts to maintain domestic law by pursuing offenders against official secrecy through foreign courts, as over Peter Wright's *Spycatcher*, the costs incurred include damage to Britain's image as an open and liberal society. The *Spycatcher* case, and the disagreements between the government and the BBC over the presentation of news and current events, attracted extensive and adverse comments in the media in the United States, Australia, Canada and elsewhere, weakening respect for British institutions and for the British government as a proponent of liberal values in international relations.

Public support for, or dissent over, a government's foreign policy is important to the strength or weakness of the positions held, being closely observed by representatives of other governments. The absence of any explicit reformulation of Britain's foreign policy priorities has left public attitudes uncertain on most aspects of foreign policy except defence. A steady 65–70% of those asked in opinion polls in recent years have agreed with the proposition that it should continue to possess nuclear weapons as long as the Soviet Union has them, with some 25–30% holding that Britain should be prepared to dismantle its nuclear deterrent before then. The British public in general provides firm support for strong national defence, though – perhaps unsurprisingly – there is no evident support for any further increase in defence expenditure and a substantial predisposition in favour of cuts. A similar spread of attitudes comes out of opinion poll data on South Africa and the commitment to help poorer countries, where clear majorities for a policy of declared opposition to the present South African government and for acceptance of the principle that developed countries have responsibilities to help underdeveloped ones coexist with a willingness to contemplate further cuts in Britain's overseas aid budget.[13]

There is no consensus, however, on Britain's preferred international partners, and much evidence of cynicism both about the transatlantic connection and the European. A long-term decline in respect both for the American way of life and for American policies is evident in polling over the past ten years. When Gallup first asked the question 'Do you think the British would be better off if they were more like the Americans?' in 1942, nearly half replied yes. Asked again in 1984 the answers divided 24% yes, 67% no, 10% no opinion. Even before Mr Gorbachev became leader of the Soviet Union there was a widespread feeling among the British public that, in terms of moral standing, the two superpowers were roughly equal. By 1987 successive polls and polling questions indicated a greater willingness to accept Soviet foreign policy at its face value than American, with, for example, 50% believing that the Soviet Union would live up to arms control agreements when signed, as against 40% for the United States, and over 50% disapproving of the US role in world affairs as against some 40% disapproving of the USSR's role.

Attitudes to Western Europe were equally ambivalent. Britain came consistently second after Denmark in *Eurobarometer* polls of

98

national opinion on the European Community in scepticism about further moves towards integration, and in lack of awareness of developments within the EC. Only 38% considered membership to be a good thing 'in the light of Britain's future in the next 10 or 15 years', even though a narrow majority considered it unrealistic for Britain to withdraw from membership. Hostility was directed particularly towards France, perceived as the dominant country in blocking the development of policies acceptable to Britain, though a majority saw Germany, accurately, as the EC's dominant economy.[14]

Concern to re-establish a sense of national identity in a multicultural society has recently led to a debate over the teaching of British history within the context of the new national curriculum. The history of the English-speaking peoples, which sustained the Churchillian consensus on Britain's postwar role, has given way over the past twenty years to a variety of approaches to British, European and world history, providing only an uncertain guide to Britain's place in the world or its past and future role. The argument is fairly made that 'a nation's knowledge of its history shapes its future' so that 'events which have created the nation we live in ... should be the very core of the core' of the national curriculum.[15] The rediscovery and re-emphasis of Britain's common heritage is therefore urged as a means of promoting social cohesion and national integration, and thus of re-creating a sense of national purpose. But the old national history may no longer be appropriate to the circumstances of the 1990s, with Britain increasingly integrated internationally, and with the growing need to teach the rising generation about the Asian countries, which will be playing an increasingly important part on the international scene, as well as to educate British citizens about the European context, which traditional English history has underplayed.

By definition, national history and national identity are inextricably intertwined. But it is difficult to write national history if there is no real sense of national identity ... Until the politicians are more clear and more agreed as to where we are going to, it is not easy for the historians to tell them where we have come from. It is difficult for a nation with no vision of its future to have a sense of its own past.[16]

Self-consciousness about the links between the teaching of national history and a sense of national identity has been most evident in Germany and Japan. Their governments are painfully aware of the immediate implications for foreign policy, as well as for domestic consensus, of historical reinterpretation. The debate over national history in Britain has not yet become so self-conscious; the sense of historical continuity has allowed the proponents of a more deliberately national curriculum to avoid the awkward issues of reinterpretation which Britain's changing international position and less certain national identity now pose. If Britain must adjust to a more Europe-centred international role how far, for example, should the traditional distinctions between English history and European history be dismantled, to emphasize the essentially European context of British history until the end of the Napoleonic Wars? As we adjust to a maturing Asian population among our citizens, how should the presentation of our national tradition treat the historical involvement of Britain in Asia? As the Asian-Pacific region becomes more and more important in the international system, ought the curriculum to pay greater attention to Asian history and culture, in addition to its established English and European foundations?

The domestic debate
Public debate, and thus public information and education, is a necessary part of rebuilding a broad domestic consensus on Britain's future international priorities. The very continuity of Britain's historical legacy, the absence of any sharp breaks in the evolution of policy – even after the Suez invasion, the collapse of the first EC application, or the eventual British accession to the EC – have made it more difficult for the public at large to appreciate the cumulative transformation of Britain's international environment over the past forty years, let alone to anticipate the further changes which are likely to occur within the next ten.

Moreover, the British political system is not well designed for informed debate on awkward issues. Parliamentary debates on foreign affairs cover points of detail, rather than of principle; the House of Commons Foreign Affairs Committee, without front-benchers from either government or opposition, plays a useful but marginal role. Uncertainties within the Labour Party over defence priorities, over the implications of remaining within the European Community and over the long-term evolution of transatlantic relations have also inhibited debate. The recovery of self-confidence has led to a stronger articulation of national interests, even of nationalism, within Parliament and in the popular press. But this has not led to any consistent criticism of the processes of industrial, financial, technological and social integration, which are blurring the outlines of the British state. It is symbolic of the contradictions between popular and political support for a more *British* identity and continued acceptance of increasing interdependence that the most stridently nationalistic British newspaper is owned by an American-Australian communications conglomerate, while the publicly owned BBC is under attack for failing to promote a sufficiently national perspective.

The management of foreign policy does not help to clarify the issues at stake. The provision of information to Parliament has declined over the past fifty years; Diplomatic Blue Books no longer appear, official secrecy is more tightly applied. The Diplomatic Service has adjusted to the frequent gap between domestic acceptability and international necessities by stressing the advantages of 'quiet diplomacy'. 'Much of our foreign policy is conducted on the sly', one senior official recently admitted, 'for fear that it would raise hackles at home if people knew what we were pushing for.' The risks of such an approach are that the gap between domestic assumptions and international negotiations may become unbridgeable in a crisis.

The management of the Falklands issue in the years before 1982 provides a classic example of the problems of such a stealthy approach. Over a fifteen-year period British governments had held inconclusive consultations with Argentina, and equally inconclusive consultations with the Falkland Islanders. The existence of a small 'Falklands lobby' in the House of Commons discouraged successive FCO ministers from explaining the dilemmas which faced them, or presenting MPs with a choice of priorities between the commitment of extra financial and military resources, and acceptance that without these sovereignty must become open to negotiation. An uninformed Parliament and an insufficiently considered drift of government policy led to a position where by late 1981 the British government had adopted an attitude towards Argentina which its own ambassador in Buenos Aires described as 'to have no strategy at all beyond a general Micawberism'.[17] The failure either to prepare parliamentary opinion for the further concessions which were the only logical conclusion of government policy, or to generate support within Whitehall and Westminster for an alternative course led both to the invasion of April 1982 and to the eruption of outraged nationalism which it provoked.

Political and official management of policy towards the European Community has exhibited from the outset a similar gap between the underlying thrust of diplomacy and the public presentation. Harold Macmillan chose to play down to a doubtful Conservative Party the significance of the shift that the first application implied, referring to the 'Common Market', rather than to the European Community, and emphasizing the continuity of British commitments to the special relationship and the Commonwealth. Such a minimalist public interpretation fed the suspicions of the French and contributed to the collapse of the negotiation. Lord Carrington's discreet enthusiasm for the strengthening of EPC in 1980–81 led to agreement among ministers on the 'London Report', setting out tighter procedures for consultation and agreement. But with the further proposals of the Genscher-Colombo Plan British diplomatic efforts were made to ensure that the final document should be termed a 'Declaration' rather than an 'Act' or a 'Treaty', thus avoiding the necessity for a public ratification process in Parliament. Similarly, in 1984, the Prime Minister's imaginative memorandum, *Europe: the Future*, which set out for the other Community governments the British government's priorities after the settlement of the budget dispute, was freely available from British embassies on the Continent, but quietly lodged in the House of Commons library in London, successfully avoiding publicity in Britain. Yet an uninformed Parliament and an uneducated public provide a weak foundation for foreign policy in a changing international context.

Among the domestic resources needed to support a more informed public debate on foreign policy – and to pursue the objectives agreed in interaction with other countries – are skills in foreign languages, and economic and political expertise on foreign countries. The US government responded to the shocks of Afghanistan, Iraq and Poland by putting additional funds into centres of Soviet studies, with its efforts reinforced by major private foundations. Federal funds currently support some ninety-three university centres of international or regional studies, as well as providing fellowship support for students to acquire the needed languages and to study in their countries of specialization.[18] 'Internationalization' has become a guiding concept in governmental and corporate priorities in Japan, leading to both a sharp rise in investment in foreign language teaching and the accumulation of necessary expertise about the international economy and about foreign societies and governments.

The creeping internationalization of Britain has been accompanied, in contrast, by a reduction in language teaching in schools, and a sharp cut-back in centres of expertise in universities – only partly reversed after a vigorous campaign by those affected and their clients in the City of London, the corporate sector and Whitehall. The uncertainty and lack of direction of government policy on international education and research – in contrast to the policies pursued in these areas by Britain's main competitors – appear to indicate yet again an underlying ambivalence over Britain's place within an increasingly interdependent world, and over the proper role of the British government in mediating between its domestic society and economy and the international environment within which they are entangled.

7
CONSTRAINTS
AND CHOICES

The radical approach which Britain's Conservative government has adopted to the conventional wisdoms and habitual patterns of domestic politics has not yet been extended to the field of foreign policy. With some few exceptions, the Thatcher government's foreign policy has been based on the assumption of continuity. Economic recovery was to enable Britain to regain the international position it was in danger of losing ten years ago, in a world not greatly changed since then. The alternative perspectives offered by the Left have, meanwhile, become ever more anachronistic, calling for Britain to exercise a moral leadership on the international stage which there is no evidence that other countries will any longer wish to follow, and talking of a national context for economic policy and for defence which takes little account of the shrinkage of British autonomy brought about by technological and economic developments.

We have to start from the world as it is, and as it is likely to be over the next ten years and more – not with the world as we remember it, or as we would have liked it to be. Self-confidence needs to be firmly rooted in a recognition of the limits of national power and of the areas where freedom of manoeuvre is possible. A heroic past is an important cement for a nation's sense of identity. But nations with an imperial past which have happily avoided the catastrophes of defeat, invasion or revolution risk continuing with illusory ambitions and overstretched international responsibilities. In the course of the 1990s the proportion of the British electorate for whom World War II and its aftermath were formative experiences will decline from a third to a quarter and less. New voters will have learned about Harold Macmillan, even about Harold Wilson, in the same way that they learned about Disraeli or Lloyd George. They will visit the sites of the Normandy landings with the same historical curiosity with which they pass by the battlefields of the Somme (neatly signposted for touring motorists on the Paris-Brussels motorway) or stop to admire the Wellington Museum at Waterloo. The completion of the Channel Tunnel and the establishment of a single internal market within Western Europe will also affect the attitudes of those born in the 1970s, who will become voters in the 1990s. When the train from London to Brussels takes no longer than the train from London to Edinburgh, and presents no greater difficulty, the sense of 'abroad' – of the sharp distinction between Britain and the European continent – will be much diminished.

Dominant powers can to a degree impose their preferred patterns on international developments, as Britain managed to do on extra-European issues in the late nineteenth century. Second-rank powers, even successful ones, need to look for opportunities at the margin, to seek to pursue their national interests in ways which do not cut too sharply across the preferences of their partners or the trends of economic and political developments. The clearer their sense of their preferred objectives and of the external pressures under which they are forced to pursue them, the better their chances of success. They need first an appreciation of the constraints under which they operate, which will clarify the choices that they are free to consider.

Constraints
The shadow of the past hangs heavily over British foreign policy, shaping the intellectual and emotional framework within which it is made and discouraging policy-makers from looking to the future. The balance of the international economy has altered very considerably in the past twenty years, while the structure of international security has remained remarkably stable. The prospect of significant evolution in international security relations during the course of the 1990s, alongside continuing rapid changes in economic relations and in patterns of finance and industrial production, increases the likelihood of a systemic transformation, which might lead away from the postwar stalemate to alternative frameworks for global cooperation and competition.

The parameters for British foreign policy in the 1990s will be set by the international system within which its policy-makers operate. We have suggested above that the likely directions of change include some real progress towards detente between East and West, accompanied by a reduction in the American commitment to Europe and increased Soviet preoccupation with domestic political and economic concerns. Western Europe seems likely to move some distance towards greater integration, including not only 'completion' of the Community's internal market but also steps towards closer coordination of financial and economic policies (including quite possibly progress towards a European central bank) and some integration of security and defence policies. The evolution of Eastern Europe will be much more problematic – a major preoccupation for Western Europe as well as the Soviet Union. Instability in the Middle East and North Africa will be as immediate a concern for Western Europe as instability in Central and Latin America is for the United States. It will require active diplomacy and cooperation with other power centres – not only the United States, but also Japan, which already provides significant economic assistance, and, preferably, the Soviet Union, which is concerned about the security of its southern borders.[1]

The economic importance of East Asia will continue to grow, as other Asian countries follow Japan along the path of industrial modernization. The political dynamics of East Asia may well become more tense, with China and other regional powers beginning to challenge Japan's dominant economic position.[2] The perception of global economic cooperation and competition as revolving around three regional power centres may be modified by the preference of other Asian countries – above all, of China – for countervailing links outside East Asia, and by the ability of the major countries (the United States, the Soviet Union, Western Europe, severally and collectively) to respond. The prospect is therefore of a global system in which economic weight and political influence will be more widely dispersed, and in which the East Asian countries – both as a grouping and as competitors for influence and markets – will play a larger role.

Multilateral bargaining, even collective management, will be needed to maintain an open international economic order and to prevent local conflicts and domestic disorder from spilling over into international instability. The shift in the balance of the international economy from the United States towards East Asia – so marked a feature of the last ten years – is likely to continue through to the end of the century, with the adjustment of structural imbalances and the problems of accumulated international debt requiring strenuous negotiation. International economic relations will thus be characterized by hard bargaining as much as by open markets. Indeed, the maintenance of a liberal economic order – and of the global economic prosperity which depends upon it – will require a continuing process of bargaining (over the rules of competition and over the adjustment of national policies to international conditions) more akin to the 'liberal mercantilism' which Edmund Dell has described than to the self-balancing markets of liberal economists.[3]

British foreign policy in the 1990s will therefore be first and foremost a matter of multilateral relations, rather than of independent initiatives or national action – of making multilateralism work to the advantage of both Britain and its preferred model of international order. The British government alone can exert no significant influence over the evolution of bilateral economic relations between the United States and Japan, or over the broader interaction between the US and the rapidly growing economies of East and Southeast Asia. It can hope to exert some modest influence over the evolution of US international economic policy, in concert with the governments of other West European countries and Japan. It can exert greater influence over the evolution of German foreign economic policy, working through the framework of the European Community, and over the stance which West European governments as a group take up on global trade and financial negotiations. Britain's standing in the international financial sector will continue to allow its government to bargain independently on some issues, if that offers the best prospect of advantage. But in other sectors the choice is likely to be between sitting in on bargaining between the United States, West Germany and Japan, or working to ensure that Britain and the other major West European governments concert their policies and combine their weight in the trilateral relationship with Japan and the United States.

Bilateral relations will serve mainly to supplement such negotiations – to prepare negotiating positions, to seek out support, to build coalitions, to inform and to trade concessions on preferred national items on the crowded agenda. British representations in Washington already compete for attention with those of other governments.

107

Britain's standing in Moscow depends upon the influence its government is seen to exert in multilateral discussions within Nato, EPC and WEU, as well as in bilateral conversations in Paris, Bonn and Washington. In negotiating within the European Community Britain needs to construct coalitions; it needs to learn how to use the support of other countries to give weight to its stance. Coalition politics does not come naturally to British policy-makers, in intergovernmental relations as in domestic politics. But it is an approach essential to summitry and caucus diplomacy, which will mark the international politics of the 1990s even more than that of the 1980s, not only in West European intergovernmental negotiations, but also in international economic management and in the delicate processes of East-West diplomacy and arms control. Almost every major West European initiative in recent years has been launched by two countries: France and Germany launched the proposal to establish the G-7 process; Germany and Italy, the Genscher-Colombo Plan to reinforce EPC; and France and Belgium, the resuscitation of WEU. Only the United States, the Soviet Union and Japan retain the capacity for independent initiative on major international issues; and they in their turn are now discovering the limits to unilateral action and the advantages of multilateral bargaining.

The parameters for Britain's foreign policy will also be shaped by its domestic context. The most important domestic constraint remains economic, in terms both of the underlying international competitiveness of the British economy, and of the burden on that economy – and on its balance of payments – of expenditure on foreign policy. It is difficult to assess how far the welcome economic recovery of the past five years will be sustained into the 1990s, as domestic oil production begins to decline and international economic circumstances alter. British manufacturing output had climbed back to the level of 1979 by 1987, but it had not yet recovered the peaks reached in 1973. Indications in the first six months of 1988 suggested the reappearance of a substantial trade deficit as a constraint on domestic economic policy and a preoccupation for ministers. It had been a constant complaint of British foreign policy-makers from the end of World War II to the late 1970s, from Ernest Bevin through Harold Macmillan and Lord Gore-Booth to Sir Nicholas Henderson, that economic weakness undermined foreign policy objectives. Concern for Britain's economy must therefore be a prior condition of foreign policy in the

1990s. A strong and competitive economy will provide a firm basis for international diplomacy. A weak economy will push British foreign policy back to the traumas of the 1960s and 1970s.

The integration of the British economy into the global economy, through inward and outward investment, rising levels of trade in manufactures and services, and internationally integrated production, will require British governments to integrate national economic management and international economic negotiation. Rising trends in migration – despite the raising of barriers against extra-European immigration – in travel, in all types of communications, will continue to integrate Britain's society with those of its neighbours across the English Channel, and, less directly, with those of the other countries of the industrialized world. The loss of the distinctively national dimension in international relations is not reversible. Britain has already yielded – or lost – the capacity to act alone across a broad range of issues, partly through declining military capabilities, partly through the acceptance of binding multilateral obligations in the EC, Nato and other international entities, and partly through the integration of its economy and society with the other advanced industrial democracies.

A determinedly nationalistic government could still, in principle, restore a greater degree of autonomy to Britain, by blocking foreign takeovers, by restoring financial institutions, newspapers and manufacturing companies to British ownership, by restricting or even ending Britain's acceptance of the authority of the European Community and of European law and by adopting a Gaullist posture on international security issues. But the costs of such a policy would be severe. The French Socialist administration discovered in 1981–2 the limits of national economic autonomy within a highly interdependent European and global economy; it shifted its priorities in recognition of these external constraints when faced with the choice between adaptation or isolation. Sweden, Norway and Austria are all reconsidering their future relations with the European Community, recognizing that the political benefits they retain by remaining non-members must be balanced against the costs of non-participation in the formulation of common policies which directly affect their domestic interests.

The prosperity of London already depends as much upon its position as an international financial centre – and on its position as a focal point in international air transport – as on its position within the British domestic economy. The loyalties of the British financial and industrial elite, which will pursue its career patterns through the capitals of Europe, North America and East Asia, working in headquarters in the United States, Japan, the Netherlands, Germany, Italy or Sweden as often as on British boards, will unavoidably become more diffuse. So, to a lesser extent, will the loyalties of those whose employment depends upon Japanese technical and management skills, and who choose for their holidays between the Mediterranean countries and the Atlantic coasts of France, Spain, Portugal and Morocco. A sense of British identity will no doubt remain as full-throated an expression of popular sentiment as that which Welshmen so readily display against England in rugby internationals. But it is likely to become more confused, even contradictory, when directed towards specific issues unless it is channelled and directed by a government with a clear sense of its long-term objectives – and a clear sense, too, of those areas where it considers it vital to maintain national autonomy, as opposed to those where international integration can be readily accepted.

Public opinion, tradition, chauvinist attitudes, all these represent a powerful constraint. Governments which ignore public sentiment or overturn long-held traditions risk being rejected by the electorate. But this is not an immovable constraint. Governments themselves shape and reshape public attitudes, by explaining to their citizens the changing circumstances to which they must adapt, by calling attention to new threats, by highlighting treasured relationships and downplaying workaday ones. The government of Britain since 1979 has successfully reshaped public attitudes on domestic issues and persuaded its citizens to recognize the limitations of government capacity and the public purse. It is possible to achieve a similar transformation in popular appreciation of foreign policy, if desired. But that is a matter for choice.

Choices
Within these parameters, the options open to British policy-makers remain relatively broad, so long as they are willing to explore the limits of choice and to explain the reasons for their preferred direction of policy to their domestic public and their partner governments. The most fundamental choice is what sort of country Britain should aim to be in the 1990s and beyond. If foreign policy is the external expression of a nation's view of itself, then policy-

makers must start by clarifying that self-perception. The question which Lord Gore-Booth posed thirty years ago still needs an answer.

> What I think I have in mind is to give us (as well as possibly Ministers) some exercise in thinking of the future of this country, whether as a world power or as a busy little island engaged in trade and manufacture but relying on others to preserve its political interests. The answer is probably somewhere between the two. But in order to achieve it, should we be a bit more extravagant or a bit more economical? We probably can't deal very much with minor parsimony, though it is important as a symptom and is giving us a bad name without producing commensurate results.[4]

A sense of national purpose – self-confidence directed towards understood objectives – is the best foundation for consensus on foreign policy, as on domestic policy. The sources of national strength which a government will wish both to exploit and to reinforce through its foreign policy come from a mixture of military power, political reputation, economic weight, technological achievement and cultural distinction. But the balance among these dimensions is a crucial area for choice.

Military power or technological competitor?
Britain has long placed a greater emphasis, and spent a larger proportion of its resources, on defence than any of its major partners except the United States. On current public expenditure projections it will continue to do so well into the 1990s. Until the late 1960s it was spending disproportionately also on the symbols of civil prestige and international standing: civil aircraft, space research, civil nuclear energy. The Plowden Report of 1965 laid heavy emphasis on

> the part played by the aircraft industry in the nation's view of itself. The traditions of the industry, especially its role in the last war; the penetration of scientific frontiers that it involves; the tangible way in which it spreads the nation's name across the world; and quite simply, the inherent glamour of aeroplanes; all these combine to make the industry a symbol of Britain's aspirations.[5]

111

Disillusionment with the possibilities of British achievement in advanced civil technology, and with the first attempts at European collaboration, has justified successive cutbacks since then, leaving Britain's external expenditure even more heavily skewed towards the military dimension in an international environment where governments pursue both advantage and prestige through support for advanced civil technology, and where the utility of military power as an instrument of foreign policy is increasingly called into question.

This is a question both of self-image and of the image which Britain's partners gain of it. Commenting on the government's refusal to join the expanded European space programme in early 1988, one American observer in London concluded:

> There is a conviction among the most influential people here
> that Britain no longer has a serious industrial or technological
> future. Its role – its inevitable role, but also, they claim, its
> correct role – will be to provide services, banking and
> insurance, consultation and intelligence, luxuries (haberdasher
> and bootmaker to Madison Avenue and Wall Street?), plus
> tourism for the Japanese and Americans. This is "little Eng-
> landism" with a vengeance.[6]

The Japanese perspective on Britain (as on the United States) is not dissimilar: it sees a civilized country in genteel decline, investing its resources in the symbols of past glory rather than in the foundations of future success, and needing the entrepreneurial skills and technological orientation of investors from abroad to carry through the economic modernization which its own society is no longer capable of sustaining. Unfair, perhaps, and over-cynical, but a characteristic response from a society which has sought – like others now following its example – to find its external expression and international standing in economic and technological advance more than in the traditional standards of national power. It may be, in the world of the 1990s, that effective international actors will need a coherent industrial strategy at least as much as a coherent military posture.

Sovereignty or integration?
There are related options in the pace and pattern of Britain's adjustment to international integration over those areas in which its

112

government might seek to reverse international trends and maintain British sovereignty, as against those in which it might consider the national interest to be best served through greater integration across national boundaries. The position of Britain as an international investor and a host to multinational enterprises from across the industrialized world has almost foreclosed the option of limiting the further internationalization of the British economy. We have, however, noted in Chapter 4 the different emphasis of government policy in the industrial and financial sectors; in the latter, unlike the former, a commitment to reciprocity and to the protection of the core of the British financial system from foreign control attempts to set limits to internationalization.

In the military field the question of how far and how fast procurement, and conventional and nuclear forces become integrated into a common security effort, or are held back as essential to national autonomy, also offers limited but real alternatives. The choices may prove most acute in the nuclear sphere. The independence of Britain's deterrent has for nearly thirty years depended upon the support of the United States and the stable framework of the Atlantic Alliance. The shift in the political geography of Western security which would follow from any substantial withdrawal of American forces from central Europe and from a lower degree of tension between the two blocs would throw into sharper relief the role of the British deterrent in European security, and the attractions – and difficulties – of closer collaboration with Western Europe's other nuclear power.

In the British debate over the first application to join the European Community a great deal was made in Parliament of the incompatibility of Britain's constitutional principles of parliamentary sovereignty with the Treaty of Rome – to the puzzlement and consternation of Continental governments, which saw this as an essentially symbolic issue outside the realities of detailed intergovernmental cooperation. In adjusting to further social and economic integration in the 1990s, Britain may face similar issues of symbolic significance, which appear to threaten its national traditions and integrity. This is a predicament it shares with all other industrialized countries to a greater or lesser degree – but that does not, of course, make its resolution any simpler.

The passionate resistance to fiscal harmonization within the European Community, as well as to the formal linking of the sterling exchange rate to the mechanisms of the EMS, demonstrates the difficulties which arise when national sovereignty as well as national interest is seen to be at stake. The introduction of a common-format, machine-readable European passport, in response to the lowering of internal Community barriers and to the rising tide of travellers flowing across its borders, brought impassioned protests in the House of Commons in May 1988 about 'the loss of the British passport', including the resounding declaration from a Conservative MP that 'the day of the nation-state is not yet over.' In response the Foreign Secretary reassured MPs that the new passport 'will remain a British passport issued under the royal prerogative' – retaining the symbols of sovereignty rather as the different badge and bonnet design retains the Bentley symbol on a Rolls-Royce car.[7] Alongside this, and in contrast, the Home Secretary was engaged in multilateral negotiations on the practical issues of national auto-nomy and intergovernmental collaboration in protecting citizens from illegal immigrants, drugs traffic, terrorism, and the internation-alization of crime – weighing up the advantages and disadvantages of maintaining Britain's national border controls in the face of the growing flood of border-crossings, and evaluating the long-term implications of closer cooperation among police forces and security agencies Europe-wide.

What strategy in Europe?

During the long debates over British accession to the European Community there was much discussion of the choice posed for the United Kingdom between the Atlantic connection and the Con-tinental commitment. That is no longer a real choice. Britain has again become a European country. The heroic era of seaborne expansion has left behind a wealth of extra-European links, and a romantic vision of a special British role in which, as Anthony Eden proclaimed in 1952, 'Britain's story and her interests lie beyond the continent of Europe. Our thoughts move across the seas . . .' But our goods and our people now move predominantly across the Channel, even though our political affections, our family links and our financial ties are more widely dispersed. The European framework for British foreign policy is no longer an alternative to extra-European priorities, but a necessary foundation for them. The link between the United States and Western Europe is no more special or vital to Britain than to Federal Germany; and it is Federal Germany, rather than Britain, which is the USA's most important partner in Western Europe. Spain, Portugal, France, Italy and the Netherlands all in their own ways retain and cultivate their active extra-European links, with higher levels of trade in several instances with such countries as Japan, China and the Soviet Union.

Once the European context is taken as given, however, a range of options for further consideration opens up. Should a British government consider it vital to play an active role in shaping the future direction of European cooperation; or should it do its best to retain a degree of autonomy and capacity for independent action, leaving to its Continental neighbours the initiative in defining the rules of European cooperation? The first alternative assumes that Britain must maintain its place alongside France and Federal Germany as a major West European power; the second that Sweden and Switzerland, or perhaps even Spain, are more appropriate, and less costly, role models for a Britain that is no longer a European power, but rather 'a busy little island engaged in trade and manufacture but relying on others to preserve its political interests'. What structures for West European cooperation does Britain seek for the future? How much effort, and how much by way of resources, should Britain devote to capitalizing on its strengths and its position within Europe to cultivate particularly close relations with extra-European states? Which extra-European states should be seen as of particular importance and advantage to British interests? How actively should the British government combine its efforts with those of its major West European partners in seeking to stabilize and strengthen the international order? Which pattern of international order should it attempt to work towards?

Britain's present government has already committed itself in principle to move with its Continental partners much further towards an integrated West European political and economic system. The Single European Act, which the British Parliament ratified in 1987, affirms in its preamble 'the will ... to transform relations as a whole among their states into a European Union', including 'the progressive realization of economic and monetary union' and the 'endeavour jointly to formulate and implement a European foreign policy'.[8] The WEU *Platform on European Security Interests* of October 1987, in the drafting of which British officials and ministers had played an active part, reaffirms in its preamble

115

'our commitment to build a European union in accordance with the Single European Act, which we all signed as members of the European Community. We are convinced that the construction of an integrated Europe will remain incomplete as long as it does not include security and defence.'[9]

However, the strength of the British government's commitment to these objectives remains open to doubt and their acceptability to Parliament is also in question. It may well be that the commitment of other Community governments may similarly prove to be weak. But there is a possibility, particularly if the next American administration takes active steps to adjust established security and economic relations with Western Europe and Japan, that the period from 1987 to 1992 will witness a surge forward in West European cooperation comparable with that which took place between 1957 and 1962.

If so, Mrs Thatcher's government, like that of her predecessor, Harold Macmillan, will have to reconsider carefully the balance of Britain's international commitments and the costs and benefits to British interests of actively working to shape these new developments, of following the lead provided by others, or of standing aside. Standing aside would indeed mark a more radical departure from the traditions of British foreign policy than active involvement; Britain is, after all, a country with broad interests, which expects to exert influence both in international security issues and in the management of the international economy. Without a coherent and actively pursued British strategy, the structure and rules of a more integrated Western Europe will be determined primarily by France and Federal Germany. These two will also play the leading role in bargaining on behalf of European interests with the United States and Japan, and in developing the European response to changes in East-West relations.

With the United Kingdom fully committed, the fulcrum for West European cooperation and for West European diplomacy towards third countries will eventually be the triangular relationship between London, Paris and Bonn. However, the successful development of such a triangular relationship requires British ministers to invest as much significance, both practical and symbolic, in their links with Bonn and Paris as in their links with Washington. It also requires the British government to clarify its objectives on the future develop-

ment of Western Europe after 1992, and to build support for those
objectives both at home and abroad.

How active a global diplomacy?
A firm West European base leaves open the option of an active
global diplomacy, combining the efforts of the major West
European states with a particular emphasis on British interests and
concerns. Shared language and historical and cultural links will
continue to provide the foundation for a higher degree of influence
in Washington than Britain's economic weight or political standing
would on their own permit. Similar social and cultural ties could
provide the basis for a continuing network of mutual influence and
advantage within the Commonwealth. Many of its African and
Caribbean member states, it is true, have structural weaknesses in
both their societies and their economies which severely limit their
usefulness and their capacity to respond; but Australia, Canada,
India, Malaysia and Singapore, for example, all have growing
economies and regional political significance. Such an option would,
however, require the investment of additional resources – in diplomatic representation, ministerial attention and travel, and government support for trade with the more highly protected and politi-
cized of these economies – for benefits which must unavoidably be
uncertain.

More certain benefits would flow from the exploitation of
Britain's links with East Asia. Britain should, therefore, encourage
Japan to see the United Kingdom as its most natural *interlocuteur* in
the Japan-Western Europe relationship, as well as its most natural
European partner in technological and financial collaboration; it
should build on the agreement over Hong Kong to develop closer
economic and political ties with China; it should draw on the
advantages of historical connection and of the predominance of
English as the international language in relations with ASEAN.

How much should Britain spend?
The question of the appropriate level of expenditure on foreign
policy has been a recurrent theme throughout this paper. A British
government committed to reducing the role of the state has the
option of making substantial savings over the next ten years –
cutting back on defence expenditure in the same way that
expenditure on overseas aid and cultural diplomacy has been cut

back – to concentrate on Britain's immediate interests without being beguiled by 'woolly' arguments about 'international responsibilities' or 'Britain's wider role'. Liberal economists of the classical school, who associated the concentration of state power with mercantilism and who assumed a close link between peaceful international cooperation and free trade, would naturally approve.

A reduction in defence expenditure, as well as in government support for industry in international competition and for the prestigious preoccupations of diplomacy, would permit a significant further reduction in the burden of taxation. The steady increase in defence expenditure from 1979 to 1986, it should be noted, was an important factor in preventing the government from achieving its objective of reducing the overall proportion of taxation to national income. The international interests of Spain and Italy are, after all, effectively promoted at much lower levels of public expenditure. The rationale for a heavier British burden has therefore to be carefully examined.

A more active European and global diplomacy, which is what we advocate, cannot, however, be effectively pursued without providing the budgetary means necessary to achieve the objectives set. The 'minor parsimony' of which Lord Gore-Booth complained thirty years ago is likely, now as then, to give Britain 'a bad name without producing commensurate results'. The worst policy to pursue is one of power without resources, of global influence on the cheap, with respect both to Britain's security and defence commitments and to its diplomatic and political role. British foreign policy since the war has seen successive governments attempting to maintain international responsibilities without the resources necessary to meet them, leaving a widening gap between aspirations and expenditure. Both the Suez action and the drift into the Falklands crisis were marked by failure to reconcile budgetary pressures and political ambitions. British defence commitments and diplomatic ambitions will face the same widening gap in the next few years unless positive steps are taken either to reduce commitments or to increase expenditure.

Stealth or openness?
There are implicit choices to be made between stealth and openness in the presentation of British foreign policy to its domestic and international audiences. Quiet diplomacy – the attempt to avoid public discontinuities by not admitting, even to the government's

parliamentary supporters, the longer-term implications of the policies pursued – has, as we have argued, characterized the conduct of British foreign policy. There is now a structural contradiction, not only between the logic of international industrial and economic integration and the national framework of popular loyalty and democratic accountability (as noted in Chapter 4), but also between the increasing integration of defence and security policies and the underlying rationale of the nation-state. The force of this contradiction has not yet filtered through to the British electorate. An increasing proportion of front-benchers on both sides of the House of Commons are, however, uncomfortably aware of the gap between the rhetoric they feel obliged to use and the realities they face in government. That gap will widen over the next ten years unless the government either takes deliberate steps to interrupt the process of integration or works with other governments to develop international structures which can attract a degree of legitimacy and provide some indirect sense of accountability.

The political obstacles to this are high: they involve governments admitting to their electors that they have lost effective sovereignty, and that they must either seek to re-establish political controls in combination with others on a Europe-wide basis or accept that Britain now looks forward to ever-decreasing influence over its own future. But the costs of avoiding a choice will also be high, beginning with an increasing degree of unreality about the domestic debate on British foreign policy. The greater the extent of popular understanding of the constraints under which the national government now operates, the greater the chances of mobilizing the support necessary for the successful pursuit of British interests through the intricate processes of multilateral bargaining which will characterize foreign policy in the 1990s.

NOTES

Chapter 1

1 Kenneth Younger, *Changing Perspectives in British Foreign Policy* (London: Oxford University Press, 1964), p. 129.
2 *Ibid.*
3 *Ibid.*, p. 89.
4 *Ibid.*

Chapter 2

1 We are grateful to Christopher Hill for drawing our attention to Acheson's fuller remarks, less often remembered.
2 Published in *The Economist*, 2 June 1979.
3 Central Policy Review Staff, *Review of Overseas Representation* (London: HMSO, 1977), p. ix.

Chapter 3

1 For more details on the current value of the Commonwealth for Britain, see Dennis Austin, *The Commonwealth and Britain*, Chatham House Paper 41 (London: RIIA/RKP, 1988).

Chapter 4

1 *OECD Main Economic Indicators*, May 1988, provides comparative growth figures up to and including 1987. The OECD's *Annual Survey for the UK, 1987*, provides trade figures only up to 1985.
2 *OECD Country Survey of UK, 1986–7*. Twenty years earlier, when European and Asian competition had been weaker, the figure was 15%.

3 *Lloyds Bank Economic Bulletin*, February 1988.
4 Stephen E. Thomsen, *The Growth of American, British and Japanese Direct Investment in the 1980s*, RIIA Discussion Paper 2 (London: RIIA, 1988). See also DeAnne Julius and Stephen E. Thomsen, *Foreign Direct Investment among the G-5*, Discussion Paper 8 (London: RIIA, 1988).
5 Robert D. Putnam and Nicholas Bayne, *Hanging Together: The Seven-Power Summits* (London: Sage, 1987).
6 DeAnne Julius, 'Britain's changing international interests: economic influences on foreign policy priorities', in *International Affairs*, Summer 1987, pp. 303–4.
7 Margaret Sharp and Claire Shearman, *European Technological Collaboration*, Chatham House Paper 36 (London: RIIA/RKP, 1987), p. 109.
8 Speech to Foreign Press Centre, Tokyo. This paragraph draws on William Wallace, 'What price independence? Sovereignty and interdependence in British politics', *International Affairs*, Summer 1986, and on John Stopford and Louis Turner, *Britain and the Multinationals* (Chichester: Wiley, 1985).
9 Martin Wolf, *The Financial Times*, 18 February 1988, reviewing *The Politics of Economic Interdependence* by Edmund Dell. He continues, 'Since Mr Dell's "autonomy" usually means the ability of the state to interfere in the transactions of its citizens with foreigners, why should they prefer such autonomy to their own?'
10 Charles Kindleberger, *American Business Abroad* (New Haven: Yale University Press, 1969), p. 207.
11 Richard N. Cooper, 'Economic Interdependence and Coordination of Economic Policies', in R.W. Jones and P.B. Kenen, eds., *Handbook of International Economics* (Elsevier: North-Holland, 1985), p. 1212.
12 Speaking on 'The Future of the Industrial Democracies' in Pittsburgh, 11 November 1975. The 1973 'linkage' debate is discussed in William Wallace, 'Issue linkage among Atlantic governments', *International Affairs*, Spring 1976.
13 Melvyn B. Krauss, *The New Protectionism: The Welfare State in International Trade* (New York University Press, 1978), p. 410.
14 Peter Ludlow, *The Making of the European Monetary System* (London: Butterworth, 1982), pp. 217–24.
15 Cooper, *op. cit.*, p. 1227.
16 Alan Clark, quoted in *The Times*, 14 February 1986; Paul Channon, quoted in *The Financial Times*, 11 May 1984.
17 Speaking at the Royal Institute of International Affairs, 5 March 1986.
18 *Striking a Balance: The Role of the Board of Trade, 1786–1986* (London: HMSO, 1986), p. 36.
19 Reprinted in *Bank of England Quarterly Bulletin*, Autumn 1987.

20 *The Times*, 7 March 1986; *The Financial Times*, 11 March 1986.
21 *The Financial Times*, 7 March 1988.
22 MoD, *Statement on the Defence Estimates, 1988*, Cm. 344–1 (London: HMSO, 1988), p. 37.
23 Robert Gilpin, *The Political Economy of International Relations* (Princeton: Princeton University Press, 1987), p. 219.
24 William R. Cline, *Reciprocity: A New Approach to World Trade Policy?* (Washington: Institute for International Economics, 1982), p. 9.
25 Kenichi Ohmae, *Triad Power: The Coming Shape of Global Competition* (New York: Macmillan, 1985), sets out this model very vigorously. Mr Ohmae is the managing director of the Tokyo office of McKinsey and Company, the international consultants.
26 Douglas E. Rosenthal and William M. Knighton, *National Laws and International Commerce: The Problem of Extraterritoriality*, Chatham House Paper 17 (London: RIIA/RKP, 1982), explores the underlying issues at stake here. See also Sharp and Shearman, *op. cit.*
27 James Eberle and Helen Wallace, *British Space Policy and International Collaboration*, Chatham House Paper 42 (London: RIIA/RKP, 1987), p. 64.
28 Speech to the Foreign Press Association, 15 May 1956.
29 Foreign Office Memorandum to Permanent Under-Secretary, 11 September 1957; PRO reference FO 371/129314.
30 CPRS, *op. cit.*, para. 2.31.
31 Paul Kennedy, *The Rise and Fall of the Great Powers* (New York: Random House, 1988).
32 See, for example, Toshiki Tomita, 'Memorandum on International Public Goods', *Tokyo Club Progress Report* (Tokyo: Nomura Research Institute/London: RIIA, 1987). On the broader issue of Britain's external budget, see William Wallace, 'Public Expenditure: The International Dimension', in M.S. Levitt, ed., *New Priorities in Public Spending* (Aldershot: Gower, 1987).
33 I.C.R. Byatt, 'Comment on the International Dimension of Public Expenditure', in *ibid.*, p. 122.

Chapter 5
1 See the discussion in Nobutoshi Akao, ed., *Japan's Economic Security*, (London: RIIA/Gower, 1983).
2 MoD, *The United Kingdom Defence Programme: The Way Forward*, Cmnd. 8288 (London: HMSO, 1981).
3 *Statement of the Defence Estimates 1988, op. cit.*, paras 106, 108.
4 *Hugh Seton-Watson Memorial Lecture*, Centre for Policy Studies, London, 28 January 1988; reprinted in *Independent*, 4 February 1988.
5 Michael Howard, 'Russia rethinks the Revolution', *The World Today*, November 1987.

6 Nato, *The Atlantic Alliance, Future Tasks of the Alliance* (Washington: USGPD, 1968), para. 9. Known as Harmel Report.
7 *Ibid.*, para. 8.
8 Speech to the Royal Institute of International Relations, Brussels, 16 March 1987; reprinted in collected speeches by the Foreign Secretary, *East-West Relations: Realism, Vigilance and an Open Mind* (London: HMSO, 1987).
9 Robert E. Hunter, 'Will the United States remain a European power?', *Survival*, May-June 1988. See also David Calleo, *Beyond American Hegemony: The Future of the Western Alliance* (New York: Basic Books, 1987).
10 Philip Windsor, 'The Middle East and Terrorism', and Christopher Hill, 'The Political Dilemmas for Western Governments', in Lawrence Freedman et al., *Terrorism and International Order*, Chatham House Special Paper (London: RIIA/RKP, 1986).
11 MoD, *Statement on the Defence Estimates, 1987*, Cm. 101-1, para. 104.
12 William Wallace, 'European Security Cooperation: The Wider Context', in Yves Boyer, Pierre Lellouche and John Roper, eds., *Franco-British Defence Cooperation* (London: RIIA/Routledge, 1988).
13 Byatt, *op. cit.*
14 *The Times*, 5 October 1987. His reference is presumably to Harold Macmillan as the last prime minister to attempt to integrate defence within a broader foreign policy; but it was the nuclear element in defence which ruined Macmillan's foreign policy objectives.

Chapter 6

1 FCO Memorandum on British Cultural Diplomacy. Reprinted in *Cultural Diplomacy*, Fourth Report to House of Commons Foreign Affairs Committee, 1986-7, para. 6.
2 'Europe: The Obligations of Liberty', Winston Churchill Memorial Lecture, Luxembourg, 18 October 1979; FCO News Department text.
3 *Cultural Diplomacy*, p. 250.
4 *UK-Soviet Relations*, House of Commons Foreign Affairs Committee (London: HMSO, 1986), p. 387-8.
5 Memorandum by BBC External Services for House of Commons Foreign Affairs Committee, reprinted in *Cultural Diplomacy*, p. 96.
6 Watching one of the new 'global' news networks available on cable in Western Europe in a Dutch hotel, one of the authors heard the announcer promise 'the best of news and entertainment from the USA, Canada, Mexico, and from foreign lands'. It should be noted that cable television and improved reception links have already given the BBC a substantial foreign audience in Belgium and the Netherlands as well as in Ireland. The BBC's late-night analysis

programme, *Newsnight*, has attracted compliments from members of the Belgian Cabinet, who claim to be among its regular viewers.

7 *House of Commons Debates*, 2 March 1988, col. 958; *Independent*, 3 March 1988.

8 Memorandum by J. Fielden on behalf of Peat Marwick, Mitchell and Co., reprinted in *Cultural Diplomacy*, p. 262.

9 Office of Population Censuses and Surveys, *OPCS Monitor*, June 1987.

10 *World Development Report 1988*.

11 Edward Mortimer, unpublished paper for Arab Thought Forum, Amman, November 1987, para. 44. He continues: 'Regrettably, however, this has had very little effect on British society or British knowledge of Arab culture. Indeed it is probable that the great majority of the British people are quite unaware of it.'

12 *OPCS Monitor*, June 1987.

13 *Gallup Political Index*, Report No. 328, December 1987, shows overseas aid (65%) and defence (48%) far ahead of all other items cited in answer to the question 'If cuts had to be made in government spending which would you choose for cuts first, and which next?'. This is of course evidence as much of the domestic preoccupations of the electorate – more concerned to protect spending on health, education, housing and support for industry – as of particular public attitudes to particular international issues. This paragraph also draws on other Gallup data of surveys in 1986 and 1987.

14 These statistics are taken from Gallup polls between August and December 1987.

15 William Rees-Mogg, 'A grasp of the past is the key to understanding the present', *Independent*, 21 July 1987. See also John Rae, 'Let democracy, prosperity and unity be the watchwords', *Independent*, 10 February 1988. The debate on the history syllabus was covered fairly extensively in The *Times Educational Supplement* and *Guardian* weekly education section over the summer of 1987.

16 David Cannadine, 'Through a glass darkly', *Listener*, 25 June 1987.

17 *Falkland Islands Review: Report of a Committee of Privy Counsellors* (London: HMSO, 1983), para. 104. Known as the Franks Report.

18 Richard D. Lambert, 'The educational challenge of internationalisation', *Washington Quarterly*, Summer 1987, p. 169.

Chapter 7

1 For details on the Soviet role in the Middle East, see Efraim Karsh, *The Soviet Union and Syria: The Asad Years*, Chatham House Paper (London: RIIA/Routledge, 1988).

2 See Laura Newby, *Sino-Japanese Relations: China's Perspective*, Chatham House Paper (London: RIIA/Routledge, 1988).

3 Edmund Dell, *The Politics of Economic Interdependence* (London: Macmillan, 1987). For an alternative view, see David Henderson, *Innocence and Design: The Influence of Economics on Policy* (Oxford: Blackwell, 1986).

4 FCO Memorandum, 11 September 1957 (as in note 29, Chapter 4).

5 *Committee of Enquiry into the Aircraft Industry, Report*, December 1965, Cmnd. 2853, p. 28. It wisely added that 'to fulfil this role, the industry must be successful'; if it produces only a string of failures, 'it will, by virtue of its symbolic role, simply exacerbate the nation's discontent and self-distrust'.

6 William Pfaff, *International Herald Tribune*, 18 February 1988.

7 *House of Commons Debates*, 4 May 1988, cols 865–6.

8 *Bulletin of the European Communities*, Supplement 2/86, pp. 5, 18; preamble and title III, article 30.

9 WEU Press Release, 27 October 1987. Title III, para. 4, it should be noted, also includes the commitment to 'see to it that the level of each country's contribution to the common defence adequately reflects its capabilities'.

Recent and forthcoming titles

The Soviet Union and Syria: The Asad Years
Efraim Karsh

This paper examines the nature of Soviet relations with Syria, assessing the commitments made and the gains reaped by Moscow and Damascus in the economic, military and political spheres. After discussing Soviet interests in the region in general and Syria in particular, the author traces the evolution of the relationship between the USSR and its main Middle Eastern ally since Asad came to power in 1970. Whilst arguing that huge military aid has intensified the pro-Soviet alignment of Syrian policy, the study contends that Asad's perception of his country's national interests has also played a large part in shaping the relationship. The author concludes that both sides have gained from what is an interdependent relationship.

Managing Exchange Rates
Peter B. Kenen

Widespread dissatisfaction with floating exchange rates has inspired new efforts to manage exchange rates among key currencies, and has also inspired proposals for the use of target zones and the adaptation of arrangements used in the European Monetary System. This paper examines the rationale for exchange-rate management, compares methods of management, and explores their implications for reserve and credit arrangements, the functioning of the IMF, the conduct of monetary and fiscal policies in the major countries and the international coordination of macroeconomic policies. The author argues that there is a compelling case for exchange-rate management but warns against reliance on half-way measures, which are corrosive of credibility.

Sino-Japanese Relations
Laura Newby

The political and economic changes that China and Japan have undergone in the 1980s have not only underlined, but also added to, the complexity of their relationship. China has seen a key role for Japan in its modernization plans, but has been disappointed by the unbalanced economic partnership formed. Japan has moved towards a higher political profile, but has not found it easy to manage politico-strategic issues with China. The evolution of the relationship in the next few years, whether towards greater integration or rising tension, will be crucial not only to regional stability and development but also to broader Western interests in East Asia.

ROUTLEDGE